MW01714760

Death Row

Death Row

PROFILES OF PEOPLE WHO
FACE THE ULTIMATE PENALTY

XAVIER WATERKEYN

NEW HOLLAND

First published in Australia in 2006 by
New Holland Publishers (Australia) Pty Ltd
Sydney • Auckland • London • Cape Town

www.newholland.com.au

14 Aquatic Drive Frenchs Forest NSW 2086 Australia
218 Lake Road Northcote Auckland New Zealand
86 Edgware Road London W2 2EA United Kingdom
80 McKenzie Street Cape Town 8001 South Africa

Copyright © 2006 in text: Xavier Waterkeyn
Copyright © 2006 in images: Newpix, Getty Images
Copyright © 2006 New Holland Publishers (Australia) Pty Ltd

All rights reserved. No part of this publication may be reproduced, stored in a retrieval system or transmitted, in any form or by any means, electronic, mechanical, photocopying, recording or otherwise, without the prior written permission of the publishers and copyright holders.

National Library of Australia Cataloguing-in-Publication Data:

Waterkeyn, Xavier.
Death row.

Bibliography.
ISBN 1 74110 387 8.

1. Capital punishment. 2. Death row. 3. Death row inmates.
I. Title.

364.66

Publisher: Fiona Schultz
Managing Editor: Martin Ford
Production: Monique Layt
Project Editor: Michael McGrath
Book Designer and Cover Photo: Greg Lamont
Picture Research: Michael McGrath, Xavier Waterkeyn
Printer: Mcphersons Printing Company, Victoria

10 9 8 7 6 5 4 3 2

Acknowledgements

Once again, I'd like to thank the team at New Holland for being so nice and accommodating. I like to give them the award for being the easiest publisher in the world to deal with. I feel blessed and very lucky. In particular I'd like to thank my editor, Michael McGrath, for being on the ball. He's done a truly sterling job.

I would also like to thank my friends and family for being so understanding when they have to put up with my testiness as I get nearer and nearer to my deadlines.

I would also like to acknowledge in debt of gratitude to everyone who helped me create *Death Row*. In particular André Kellner at Death Row Speaks, Carla Andrews at Battlecry of Innocence and to Death Row inmates William van Poyck and Milo Rose for sharing their stories with me—and you. I truly appreciate their generosity.

Contents

To the victims of crime …
and to every innocent man and woman
who ever died for crimes they did not commit.

Introduction

Capital punishment and the death sentence have been with humans since before the beginning of history. The first known record of the death penalty belongs to the famous code of Hammurabi, dating from 1750 BC, and has been a part of every civilised society since then.

In the modern world the death penalty is still very popular. According to Amnesty International, out of 196 countries, 120 are abolitionist in law or practice, but about 76 still practice execution with considerable enthusiasm and frequency. Retentionist countries include some of the largest and most powerful states in the world, including China, India, Indonesia, Japan, North Korea, South Korea, the Philippines, Saudi Arabia, Singapore, Thailand and, of course, the United States of America.

It is not hard to see why America seems to dominate the discussion of capital punishment. To start with, America has the world's largest prison population.

According to the International Centre for Prison Studies at King's College in the University of London the figure stood at 2 135 901 on 31 December 2004. Out of every 100 000 people in America 724 are housed in 3335 local jails, 1558 state facilities and 146 federal facilities. As the official maximum capacity of these facilities is less than 2 000 000 the jails are therefore currently overcrowded by 7.6 per cent. Some estimate that up to 25 per cent of all American males will have some dealings as a 'client' of the justice system at some point in there lives. Russia, by contrast, is a poor second with only 812 700 prisoners as of the first of November 2005. America is the only 'Western' democracy that has retained the death penalty. All the others abandoned it, often decades ago.

The last man hanged in New Zealand was 68-year-old farm worker, Walter James Bolton, on 18 February 1957 at Mount Eden Prison in Auckland.

The last men executed in Canada were Ronald Turpin, 29, and Arthur Lucas, 54. They were hanged in a joint execution on 11 December 1962 in Don Jail, Toronto for separate murders. In both cases the victims were policemen.

The last men executed in the United Kingdom were Peter Anthony Allen, 21 and Gwynne Owen Evans (also known as John Robson Walby), 24, who were hanged virtually simultaneously on 13 August 1964 in Liverpool and Manchester (respectively) barely four months after battering and stabbing to death 54-year-old John Alan West on 7 April 1964.

The last man guillotined in France was Tunisian immigrant, 28-year-old Hamida Djandoubi, at Baumetes Prison in Marseilles at 4.40 am on 10 September, 1977, for the torture and murder of 21-year-old Elizabeth Bousquet in July 1974.

Germany abandoned capital punishment on 24 May 1949 and has since become the most vocal opponent in Europe to the death penalty. In fact, under the European Convention on Human Rights the death penalty can never be reintroduced to any country in the European Union.

Across the Atlantic, however, opinion polls frequently cite that around 60–70 per cent of Americans still approve of the death penalty.

As of 1 October 2005, America had a Death Row population of 3383. More than 100 of these prisoners were aged over 60 and the average time spent on Death Row was over 10 years.

Of the 50 states, 38 still have the death penalty on their books. Those states are: Alabama, Arizona, Arkansas, California, Colorado, Connecticut, Delaware, Florida, Georgia, Idaho, Indiana, Illinois, Kansas, Kentucky, Louisiana, Maryland, Mississippi, Missouri, Montana, Nebraska, Nevada, New Hampshire, New Jersey, New Mexico, New York, North Carolina,

Ohio, Oklahoma, Oregon, Pennsylvania, South Carolina, South Dakota, Tennessee, Texas, Utah, Virginia, Washington and Wyoming.

The United States Federal Government and the United States Military also have the death penalty, although the Navy hasn't executed anyone since 1849.

The top three states for prisoners waiting on Death Row are California (644), Texas (441) and Florida (384). Historically—before the 10-year moratorium on executions between 1967 and 1977—the top three were Virginia (1277 executions), New York (1130) and Pennsylvania (1040). Since 1977, when executions recommenced, the top three executing states have been Texas (347), Virginia (94) and Florida (60).

These days, the overwhelmingly popular choice for execution is lethal injection. Many consider it the most humane method yet developed. Two needles are inserted into 'usable veins,' usually in the arms. The condemned is first given a 5.0 gram dose of sodium thiopental, an anaesthetic that puts the recipient to sleep. Then comes 50cc of pancuronium bromide that paralyses the breathing muscles. Finally 50cc of potassium chloride stops the heart. Death results essentially from poisoning in about 15 minutes. The cost of the chemicals is about $US87.00.

Lethal injection first became legal in Oklahoma in 1977, although the first criminal executed by injection was Charles Brooks on 2 December 1982.

The second most popular method of execution is the electric chair, invented in 1888 by Harold P Brown—an employee under the direction of Thomas Edison—as a political stunt, to prove that alternating current was deadlier than direct current. It was first used to execute William Kemmler, in Auburn prison New York on 6 August 1890, for the murder of his common-law wife, Tillie Ziegler. The execution was rather botched. The first 17-second charge only succeeded in badly burning the condemned. The second charge at 2000 volts lasted over a minute and virtually roasted the man. A reporter who witnessed the execution called it: 'an awful spectacle, far worse than hanging.'

In spite of all the shootings, hangings, gassings, electrocutions and injections over the years, it's surprising how many famous, 'Big Name' criminals were not executed.

Ed Gein, the inspiration for the movie *Psycho*, was judged insane and died of cancer, aged 78, in Waupan State Hospital on 26 July 1984.

Gangster boss Al Capone, 48, died of a heart attack, on 21 January 1947—out of jail in his mansion in Palm Island.

Serial killers Henry Lee Lucas and his partner Otis Toole were jointly responsible for over a hundred deaths. Toole, 49, died in prison in Florida on 15 September 1996, from liver failure. Lucas, 64, died in prison in Texas, of heart failure on 13 March 2001.

Necrophiliac and cannibal Jeffrey Dahmer was serving 15 consecutive life sentences in Columbia Correctional Institution in Wisconsin, a state without the death penalty. He was cleaning the bathroom on work detail when fellow inmate Christopher Scarver beat him to death on 28 November 1994.

The case of Gary Ridgway, the Green River Killer of over 48 victims, probably points to a new wave of the future, where courts are increasingly willing to enter into 'deals' with murderers: 'We won't kill you, just as long as you tell us where all the bodies are.'

Nevertheless, Death Row has still managed to claim some major players, some infamous and deadly and some obscure, but no less deadly.

Gallery of Rogues

1892–1906

The Baby Farmers of Australia

You're an unwed mother-to-be in the late 1800s. Society condemns you. Your family ostracises you. You've ruined your chances of a good marriage. Given the spirit of the age, your options are extremely limited: find a man who will marry you before your child is born (if you can find a man who will have you), have a backyard abortion and hope you don't become a cripple or die of infection, or 'visit relatives' for several months and have the child. You might find a factory job and bring up the child as an outcast in appalling poverty; or you could adopt the child out; or you could give it to a baby farmer.

Baby farms were mostly well-run places that could raise your child, for a regular fee, until you were ready to reintroduce it to your family as an orphaned 'niece', 'nephew' or 'cousin'. The child wouldn't be a bastard. You wouldn't be a whore.

There were some baby farms, however, run by people who knew they had all the power and mothers had little redress. If anything went wrong, shame and stigma would keep the mothers quiet. Unscrupulous baby farmers would take the money and either sell the baby or, if that didn't work, scrimp on the expenses until the children died of disease or neglect. That sort of thing was easy enough to hide in a world where, even with the best of care, many children didn't live past their first few years. Some baby farmers couldn't even wait that long. They turned instead to outright murder.

1892: John and Sarah Makin

Amber Murray gave birth to her son, Horace, in March 1892. She put an advertisement in the Sydney Morning Herald offering her baby up for adoption. She was prepared to pay for the child's support.

Amber met John Makin, 50, and his wife Sarah, 47, who lived in Redfern with their daughters and about half a dozen other babies they were 'minding for friends'. The Makins said they'd be happy to look after Horace for 10 shillings a week. Amber agreed to the deal as long as she could visit Horace now and then. Everything seemed fine.

John Makin called on Amber every week for the 10 shillings. Amber paid, but whenever she asked if she could see her boy he would give her an excuse, not the boy. Eventually Makin told Amber that the family were moving much farther away to Hurstville and would give Amber the details once they were finally settled. Makin nevertheless continued to call for the 10 shillings per week.

Contrary to John Makin's story the family moved only a few suburbs away to MacDonaldtown. Daughter Clarice Makin later testified that there was no sign of Horace Murray once they'd moved. In August the Murrays moved again to nearby Chippendale.

On 11 October 1892 drainer James Hanoney was working in the backyard of the MacDonaldtown house when he found two bundles of putrid smelling babies' clothing blocking an underground drain. In the clothing were the decomposing bodies of two infants. Investigating police found another five infants' bodies in the backyard.

Tenancy records allowed them to trace the Makins to the previous house in Redfern, where they found another five bodies. John and Sarah Makin and their four daughters Florence, 17, Clarice, 16, Blanche, 14 and Daisy, 11 were arrested. Police charged Mr and Mrs Makin with murder.

Large crowds attended the trial at Sydney's Supreme Court. Sarah Makin had pawned some of the babies' clothing. Amber Murray and three other mothers identified their babies' things.

One fact soon emerged. The Makins were equal opportunity exploiters. They were clever enough to extract whatever funds the parents could afford. Every little bit helped. One couple had, over time, paid the Makins money amounting to, for them, the considerable sum of two pounds, only to have the Makins later tell them that their baby had died.

The Makins couldn't keep their story straight and, as the evidence mounted, even their daughters testified against them.

In his summing up the presiding judge, Justice Stephen, referred to Horace Murray and said: ' ... you buried this child in your yard as you would the carcass of a dog ... you were carrying on this nefarious, this hellish business ... destroying the lives of these infants for the sake of gain.'

When Justice condemned the Makins to death Sara collapsed in the dock, John had to hold her up. John was hanged; Sarah's sentence was commuted. She was released in 1911—her fate is unknown. No conviction was recorded against the four Makin daughters.

1894: FRANCES KNORR

Frances Knorr was born Minnie Thwaites in London in 1868. Embarrassingly ill-disciplined and promiscuous, her family sent her to Sydney in 1887. She worked as a servant until she married German waiter and petty-criminal Randolph Knorr. They had a daughter called Gladys, but while Mr Knorr served 18 months in Pentridge Gaol for fraud, Mrs Knorr had an affair with Edward Thompson and moved to Melbourne. When the Thompson affair ended she set herself up as a child minder. She had no trouble finding clients, but never stayed too long anywhere, frequently moving and often using either the name Thwaites or Knorr.

While living in Moreland Road, Brunswick she strangled a little girl with a length of rope and buried her body in the garden. She had moved back to Sydney and was back with her husband when the new tenant of Moreland Road found the little girl's body while digging in the garden. Neighbours then led police to another house where Knorr had lived and there they found the bodies of two little boys who Knorr had suffocated.

A Detective Keating arrested her in Sydney while she was in bed, giving birth to her second child. She didn't seem surprised: 'I know what you have come for,' she said. Knorr's child was born in custody and the couple was extradited to Melbourne.

The police reports described her as '... age about 25 years, height 5ft 2in (157.4 cm), fair complexion, very stout build, light brown hair, very large peculiar-shaped mouth, very talkative and speaks with a lisp.'

While awaiting trial she wrote to Edward Thompson. Thompson's mother delivered the letter to the police soon after.

Knorr's dealings were almost impossible to keep track of. She'd swapped, passed on and traded so many children that the situation was a mess. During the inquest into the death of one of the boys—Isaac Marks, in October 1893—33 witnesses were called.

At Knorr's five-day trial the prosecution produced Knorr's letter to Thompson. It asked that he create some evidence for her defence. The letter also asked him to pay off a couple to say that they had buried a child born to Knorr and Thompson, who had died of consumption. This ploy to implicate Thompson and bring him down with her failed, so she tried to claim the children had died of natural causes. The medical evidence said otherwise.

When Justice Holroyd passed the mandatory death sentence, Knorr screamed at Thompson: 'God forgive you for your sins, Ted. God help my poor mother. God help my poor babies.'

The court appointed Thomas Jones to carry out the sentence. Although he had already hanged 15 men the idea of hanging a woman unhinged him. He took to drink and, while drunk, cut his own throat two days before Knorr's scheduled execution.

Hundreds of Melbourne citizens protested that hanging a woman and a mother was inhuman.

Inspired by the solace she found in religion during the final weeks of her life Knorr wrote this statement: 'Placed as I am now within a few hours of my death, I express a strong desire that this statement be made public with the hope that my fall will not only be a warning to others, but also act as a deterrent to those who are perhaps carrying on the same practice. I now desire to state that upon the two charges known in evidence as Number 1 and Number 2 babies, I confess to be guilty.'

On the morning of her execution she sang hymns from dawn until the moment the newly appointed executioner placed a noose around her neck. Outside Pentridge Gaol two hundred supporters also sang hymns.

Knorr's final words were clear: 'Yes, the Lord is with me! I do not fear what men may do to me, for I have peace, perfect peace!' At 10 am on 15 January 1894 she dropped 7ft 6in (2.3m) into even deeper peace. She would be the last woman hanged in Victoria until Jean Lee, 57 years later.

Based on the evidence at the inquest authorities estimated that she might have killed as many as 13 babies.

1900–1906: Alice Mitchell

Australia's most famous case of negligent or malicious baby farming was that of Alice Mitchell. More than 37 babies might have died in appalling, maggot-infested squalor while in her 'care' at various locations in Perth over a six-year period. Funeral parlours and the Council Health Department had failed to notice anything unusual. On 12 March 1907 a coroner's inquest found that the case was 'the most revolting ever dealt with. It is loathsome, disgusting, filthy and monstrous.' Yet, though many people in high places were 'severely reprimanded' and Mitchell was charged with wilful murder, the absence of evidence and witnesses brought instead a verdict of manslaughter for only one child, baby Ethel Booth.

Alice Mitchell, arguably Australia's most successful serial killer was sentenced to only five years' hard labour.

The scandal of the Mitchell case led to the State Children Act of 1907 and similar legislation in other states. The practice of baby farming is now a distant memory.

There is no record of what happened to Alice Mitchell once she was released from jail.

1896

The Factory of Death: HH Holmes

After more than a century, the legend of H H Holmes has obscured the facts; it didn't help that Holmes was a conman and a pathological liar. After his arrest, he gave conflicting and contradictory confessions of his crimes so that now we'll never know the full truth. Many mysteries still surround the case. Perhaps one of the most intriguing is: how could America's greatest serial killer be almost forgotten, a mere footnote in history? One thing seems certain though, Holmes was probably the most systematic mass murderer in modern history. Not since the famous cases of Gilles de Rais and Elizabeth Bathory, in Medieval Europe, was a killer able to dedicate an entire building to torture and murder. He makes John Wayne Gacey look like an amateur.

The monster of 63rd St was born Herman Webster Mudgett to a prominent and wealthy family in the hamlet Gilmanton Academy, in rural New Hampshire on 16 May 1860. Reports of his childhood are as conflicting and contradictory as any other stories about his life. His father, the local postmaster, was supposedly abusive and his mother, meek and religious. He left high school at 16, left home and assumed the name of Henry Howard Holmes. At 18 he married Clara Lovering and studied medicine in Burlington, Vermont, paying for his education with his wife's inheritance. In 1879 he transferred to the University of Michigan medical school in Ann Arbor. While there he took out life insurance policies on fictitious relatives, stole cadavers from the school, disfigured and disguised the corpses, put them in places where they seemed to have suffered an accident, then claimed the insurance money when the corpses were found. According to one of his later published confessions, his first murder was of a former schoolmate—committed for the insurance money. He claimed that the killing gave him an appetite for blood. He also killed people to sell their bodies to a corpse dealer: it was a common practice of the time to sell corpses to medical schools.

Holmes continued his murders and assorted frauds until one day he was caught in the act of body snatching. So he simply left town, abandoning his wife and their infant son. They never saw Holmes again. They were lucky.

In 1885 Holmes began proceedings to divorce Lovering, but the case dragged on until 1891. Unhindered by his still-unresolved divorce he married Myrtle Z Belknap, that same year. The marriage to Belknap didn't last either. She was pregnant with their daughter when she left him within a year. They were lucky too. Belknap finally divorced him in 1889.

In 1886 Holmes moved to the Chicago suburb of Englewood, where he answered an advertisement for the position of pharmacist, at Dr ES Holton's drugstore at the corner of 63rd and South Wallis Streets. Holton was dying of prostate cancer, his 63-year-old wife was barely able to cope with their customers and the handsome, charming, well-dressed and eminently able Holmes seemed a godsend. Mrs Holton hired him on the spot and Holmes was soon doing a roaring trade. After Mr Holton died, Holmes offered to buy the business. Mrs Holton agreed but, when he failed to keep up the payments, she took him to court. Then, in 1887, she disappeared. Holmes told everyone that she and her daughter had moved to California. No one ever heard from them again.

Soon after he opened a jewellery counter at the drugstore and hired Julia Connor. She and her daughter Pearl soon moved in with Holmes.

In 1888, he met Benjamin Pietzel, who was by all accounts a weak-willed alcoholic, but perfect partner in many of Holmes' cons. He also, briefly, met a woman in New York: Minnie Williams.

Holmes wasn't content just to run a successful pharmacy, even one that he had bought with murder. His scams included tapping into Chicago's water supply, flavouring tap water with vanilla, rebottling it and selling it as 'Linden Grove Mineral Water'. As was to happen so many times in his life, Holmes was caught, but not charged. Although Holmes seemed to delight in cheating people for its own sake, the fact was that he did need money and lots of it. He had plans: plans that he drew up himself. In 1889, he bought a large lot across the road from the pharmacy. In 1890 work began there on a huge, three-storey, hundred-room shopping centre, hotel and residence—Holmes Castle—which he planned to complete by the time of the upcoming Colombian Exposition of 1893. During construction he constantly hired and fired builders on any pretext he could think of. As a result, more than 500 labourers worked on the project. For Holmes this had two major advantages. One: he never paid the builders. Two: he obscured the building's true purpose.

Holmes Castle was completed in 1892. Below ground was an extensive cellar and the ground floor was dedicated to shops. The top floor was supposedly Holmes' residence, although later examination determined that it was hardly ever used. The middle floor was supposedly dedicated to hotel rooms. In reality it was a torture chamber.

The Colombian Exposition—or Chicago World's Fair of 1893—provided the perfect opportunity for Holmes to find victims. During its six month run some 27 million people visited Chicago. City and police resources were stretched to the limit. It was just the environment Holmes wanted for his peculiar brand of mayhem.

He had constructed a perfect set of covers. He would place classifed advertisements for accommodation at his hotel, want ads for his various business interests and advertisements seeking a wife. It paid to advertise. There was an almost constant stream of visitors to the fair from all over the world and there were any number of young women looking for work and opportunities. In his book *Depraved*, Harold Schechter tells us that what many of them found instead was this:

- Soundproofed bedrooms with peep holes, so Holmes could watch his victims as he tortured them.

- Asbestos-padded walls in rooms equipped with flaming gas jets.
- Airtight rooms that could be pumped with poisonous gas or simply left shut until the victims slowly asphyxiated.
- A specially equipped surgery for dissection of the dead … and the living.
- Rooms equipped with torture devices—including an 'elasticity determinator' for investigating how far the human body could be stretched
- False floors, secret passages and chutes leading to the cellar below, which contained vats of acid, a furnace and a pit filled with quicklime for dissolving, incinerating and disposing of the bodies and skeletons that Holmes chose not to sell to medical schools.

What his victims probably never saw was the secret control room from which Holmes coordinated his prolonged executions. Police traced no fewer than 50 people to Holmes Castle before their trails went cold. However, the estimates of Holmes' executions range as high as 200.

While Holmes was torturing and murdering for fun and profit he caught up again with Minnie Williams. Julia Connor became jealous of Minnie. Holmes later confessed that Julia died during a bungled abortion, but he also confessed that he 'would have gotten rid of her anyway. I was tired of her.' Pearl, he simply poisoned. Minnie in turn became jealous of an employee called Emmeline Cigrand, so Holmes raped and killed the young woman. When Emmeline's fiancé, Robert E Phelps, visited the Castle to find out what had happened to her, he simply vanished off the face of the Earth.

Not long after, using his famous charm, Holmes convinced Minnie's sister, Nettie, to sign over her worldly goods to him. Nettie promptly disappeared—although Holmes later claimed that Minnie killed her sister by bludgeoning her with a chair. Shortly after, Holmes decided that he'd had enough of Chicago. The World's fair was now over and the pickings had become lean. So Holmes set fire to the Castle, which only partially destroyed it. In the process of claiming the insurance money Holmes quit the city.

On 17 January 1894, Holmes married Georgianna Yoke in Denver. Minnie was a witness at the wedding. While on his honeymoon Holmes arranged a successful and lucrative horse swindle in Texas. Ironically, this scam would be his undoing and, in July 1894, Holmes was arrested for it.

While in jail he hit upon yet another insurance scam. Fellow inmate and convicted train robber, Marion Hedgepath, was serving a 25-year sentence when Homes offered him $500 to give him the name of a crooked lawyer. Hedgepath introduced him to Jeptha Howe. Holmes would fake his own death and collect $20 000. While free on bail, Holmes absconded and implemented his plan, but the scheme failed. Somewhere around this time though he found the opportunity to kill Minnie Williams.

He then convinced his erstwhile partner, Benjamin Pietzel, to take out a life insurance policy on himself for $10 000. Pietzel's whole family was in on it. They all agreed that they should find an anonymous corpse, burn it, identify it as Pietzel's and then claim the insurance money.

On 4 September 1894, Pietzel was lying in bed in a drunken stupor, hiding out in a hotel room on account of the scam. Holmes tied the sleeping man up, drenched him in benzene and burned Pietzel alive. Holmes took the corpse to an office and arranged for a convenient explosion. Holmes used Pietzel's 15-year-old daughter, Alice, to help identify the body 11 days later. She, like the rest of the Pietzel family, believed the body was that of a stranger. Two weeks later Jeptha Howe filed a claim on the part of the Pietzel family. Howe kept $2500—Holmes the rest. Holmes gave the widow, Carrie Pietzel, $500, but then took it back, claiming he would 'invest it for her'. In his greed Holmes also bilked Hedgepath of his money. This was Holmes' fatal mistake. Hedgepath turned him in and the insurance company engaged the Pinkerton Detective Agency to find him.

Unaware that he was now the subject of a manhunt, Holmes took Georgianna, Carrie and the children—Alice, 15, Nellie, 11, and Howard, 8, as well as Carrie's other two children—on an extended trip around the country. On 1 October 1894 Holmes sent Carrie and the two smaller children to New York. He and Georgianna also separated. Authorities later found Georgianna at her parent's house in Indiana and Carrie Pietzel in Burlington, Vermont, in a house that Holmes had rented for her. Holmes continued to travel with the other three children. Fortunately for the case—and for history—Alice and Nellie wrote letters to their mother, describing their travels with him. Holmes told Carrie Pietzel that her husband was either in South America or Florida and that her children were with a guardian, Minnie Williams, in England.

Holmes took the children to Indianapolis. While they were staying there he separated Howard from the girls. Holmes took the boy to a house in Irvington where he poisoned and dismembered him and burned the pieces. After leaving Indianapolis, Alice wrote: 'Howard is no longer with us.' Who knows what Holmes told the boy's sisters? Whatever he said, he wrote to Carrie Pietzel and asked her and her two other children to meet him in New York. He took Alice and Nellie to Chicago, Detroit and then to Toronto. There, during a game of hide and seek, the girls climbed into a trunk. Holmes proceeded to pump poison gas into it.

He planned to kill Carrie and the other two children with nitroglycerine in New York. Instead authorities arrested Holmes on 17 November 1894, in Boston, as he was preparing to leave the country by steamship. Ironically, in spite of all that he'd done, the arrest wasn't for any murder. It was for the theft of the horses in Texas. But authorities in Philadelphia were already on to him. Carrie Pietzel's flustered and confused account of her travels with Holmes and the mystery of the disappearing children convinced them that Benjamin Pietzel and the children were dead. Given the choice of hanging as a horse thief in Texas or going to Philadelphia on insurance fraud, Holmes picked Philadelphia.

For Holmes the arrest was simply another opportunity to play the game of cat and mouse that he had always played. Holmes simply told one story after another.

Initially he said that Pietzel's charred body belonged to an anonymous corpse. So on 3 June 1895 he was tried for conspiracy to defraud an insurance company. That charge kept him in jail while detective Frank Geyer began the search for the Pietzel children. Fortunately, he had with him Alice and Nellie's letters. Holmes had never mailed them and they were in his possession when the police arrested him. On 26 June 1895, guided by Alice's and Nellie's letters, funded by the insurance company and applying skilful and inspired detective work, Geyer began a months-long, highly-publicised search that finally uncovered the fate of the Pietzel children. Later Geyer wrote that: 'No less than nine hundred supposed clues were run out' in the search.

Following the leads in the letters and searching the records of recent rentals, Geyer finally discovered a house that Holmes had rented in Toronto. Digging in the soft dirt of the cellar at number 16 Vincent St he found the partially decomposed bodies of Alice and Nellie Pietzel. As workers removed Nellie's body her braid pulled her scalp away from her skull. Carrie Pietzel was later only allowed to see her children's hair and teeth as the rest of the remains were too putrefied for her to view. Nonetheless, she recognised them instantly. Only then did she realise how Holmes had lied to her.

On 24 July 1895, Geyer returned to Indianapolis. After several weeks he made it to the house in Irvington. There, in a small alcove, he found a trunk that had belonged to Carrie Pietzel. In the barn there was a coal stove stained with what looked like dried blood.

Geyer returned to Chicago. He and the police spent weeks going through the partially destroyed Castle, reconstructing its floor plan. In the cellar, among other things, they found a wooden box filled with female skeletons, a carefully wrapped ball made from women's hair and the charred remains of a watch that had belonged to Minnie Williams.

During the trial thousands of people lined up to visit 'Murder Castle' on the corner of 63rd and South Wallace.

One entrepreneur bought Murder Castle and planned to convert it into a tour-guided museum but, before it opened, it burned to the ground shortly after midnight on 19 August 1895 under 'suspicious' circumstances.

Soon after, on 27 August, a doctor examined the house in Irvington where Holmes had killed Howard. The doctor found some charred remains in the chimney. Part of the skull, a femur, a complete set of teeth, a piece of jaw and a baked stomach, liver and spleen were all that were left of Howard Pietzel.

Not to be outdone by these latest revelations, Holmes wrote a predictably false and self-vindicating memoir: *Holmes' Own Story 'in which the Alleged Multimurderer and Arch Conspirator Tells of the Twenty-two Tragic*

Deaths and Disappearances in which he is Said to be Implicated.' It didn't help that the public didn't believe him and even his third wife, Georgina Yoke, testified against him at the trial.

On 12 September 1895, a grand jury indicted Holmes for the murder of Benjamin Pietzel. Holmes changed his story again: the body suddenly became that of Pietzel after all. Holmes claimed that the man had died of 'natural causes'. In the midst of all the tall tales Holmes became less and less convincing.

By now his case had become a familiar national sensation. His trial began on 28 October 1895. True to form, he fired his lawyers and questioned the jury himself. This was a bold move and unprecedented: no accused murderer had ever done this in America before. Yet, as the trial continued in Philadelphia, more and more evidence mounted against him in Chicago.

Holmes' famous charm finally failed him. On 4 November 1895, after just five days in court and a two-hour deliberation, the jury convicted him of the first-degree murder of Pietzel. The jury later confessed that they only taken one minute to find Holmes guilty, but that they had stayed out longer 'for the sake of appearances'.

After his conviction Holmes abandoned all pretence of declaring his innocence and, for the promise of $10 000, he successfully sold his story to the Hearst group of newspapers. He reinvented himself yet again, this time as the most infamous killer in the world. He confessed to killing over 100 then changed his mind and reduced the number to 27. At that time, and for long after, he was much bigger than Ted Bundy would later be. This latest confession was published on 12 April 1896 and contained such lurid passages as:

> 'Like the man-eating tigers of the tropical jungle, whose appetite of the blood have once been aroused, I roamed about this world seeking whom I could destroy … I was born with the devil in me. I couldn't help the fact that I was a murderer, no more than a poet can help the inspiration to seem. And I was born with the evil one standing as my sponsor beside the bed where I was ushered into the world. He has been with me ever since.'

Yet Philadelphia's district attorney, George Graham, summed it all up when said: 'the confession is a mixture of truth and falsehood. Holmes never could help lying.'

They hanged him at 10:13 am on 7 May 1896—nine days before his 36th birthday—at Moyamensing prison in Philadelphia. The execution was a major public event. His last meal was boiled eggs, dry toast and coffee. His last words were: 'Take your time. You know I am in no hurry.' As he hanged it took Holmes' heart almost 15 minutes to stop beating. The report states that during that time his hands clenched and his feet jerked as the rope further embedded itself into his flesh.

Holmes was terrified that scientists would want to cut up his brain for examination and study. As per his request, his body was placed in a pine box that was then filled with cement. The coffin was buried 10 feet (3m) deep and covered with two tonnes of cement. It's still there, unmarked, in the Holy Cross Cemetery, Philadelphia.

The lot at the corner of 63rd and South Wallace in Chicago remained empty for years. In 1938, a US Post Office was built on the site. The place remained a focal point of strange tales and bizarre happenings. Residents claimed they couldn't walk their dogs on the same side of the street since the animals would invariably start whining and howling.

There were even tales of a series of deaths that followed Holmes' execution. Dr William K Matten, a witness at the trial, died suddenly of blood poisoning. The head coroner, Dr Ashbridge, and the judge who sentenced Holmes to death both contracted sudden, rare diseases. The superintendent of Holmes' prison committed suicide.

After considerable lobbying the State acknowledged that Marion Hedgepath's role in Holmes' arrest had been crucial. He was pardoned in 1906, but soon turned back to crime. On New Year's Eve 1910 police shot him as he attempted to rob a saloon in Chicago.

1910

Murder and Stupidity: Doctor Hawley Harvey Crippen

The spectacular case of Doctor Crippen created a huge sensation across the world in the first decade of the twentieth century. It kept an army of journalists busy for months trying to satisfy a public eager and greedy for more details of a bizarre murder, with an even more bizarre aftermath.

Born in Coldwater, Michigan, in 1862, Harvey Crippen went to England in 1883 to gain a medical diploma and in 1885 acquired another diploma as an eye and ear specialist in America. In 1887 he married Charlotte Belle in Detroit. They had one son, Otto, but in 1890 or 1891 Charlotte died in Salt Lake City. To the best of anyone's knowledge Charlotte died a natural death. Harvey sent his son to live with Charlotte's mother in California and he hardly ever saw the boy again.

In 1893 in New York Crippen met and married 17-year-old music hall performer, Cora Turner, whose aliases included Cora Motzki and Belle Elmore. Her real name was Kunigunde Mackamotzki. Harvey eventually worked full-time for the Munyon Company, as a homeopath, selling patent medicines while wasting money on talentless Belle's opera training.

Harvey and Belle moved to London in 1900 so that Harvey could manage Munyon's London office. He left Munyon and failed with several businesses, including the 'Drouet Institute', where he met Ethel Le Neve Harvey. He later employed Ethel as a typist when he returned to Munyon.

Harvey and Belle's marriage was not a happy one. Belle was a large, loud woman with dyed-blond hair and a domineering personality. In 1908 she started working as Honorary Treasurer of the Music Hall Ladies Guild. A friend, Adeline Harrison, described Belle as 'a brilliant, chattering bird of gorgeous plumage. She seemed to overflow the room with her personality. Her bright, dark eyes were twinkling with the joy of life. Her vivacious rounded face was radiant with smiles.' As much of a 'joy' as she might have been to her friends she was pretty hard going on her husband. She nagged him incessantly, constantly demanding, and getting, jewels and furs—'she would babble to her diamonds and kiss them.' Belle decorated the Crippen house—at 39 Hilltop Crescent, Camden Town—with pink wallpaper, pink lampshades and pink velvet ribbons on the corners of the wall paintings. She would select Harvey's clothes for him because he 'had no taste'. She even convinced Harvey to convert to Catholicism.

Harvey, on the other hand, was meekness personified. A small, bald man with prominent bespectacled eyes, his only really distinguishing feature was a heavy, sandy-blonde moustache.

The Crippens had not 'enjoyed marital relations' since 1907, but Belle's lover was the American music-hall artist Bruce Miller. Harvey had Ethel.

In December 1909 Belle decided that she'd had enough of her farcical marriage, announced that she would be leaving Harvey and taking their joint savings of £600 with her. This was equivalent to about two years of Harvey's salary.

On the evening of 31 January 1910, the Crippens entertained friends Paul and Clara Martinetti. They played whist until 1:30 am on 1 February.

It is from this point on that history remembers Harvey Crippen, not so much for his crime as for his stupidity. On 1 February, Harvey pawned some of Belle's diamond earrings and a diamond ring for £80. On 3 February, the Music Hall Ladies Guild received letters from Belle Elmore announcing her retirement as Honorary Treasurer on account of having to go to America to visit sick relatives. The letters were not in Belle's handwriting. Harvey pawned more jewellery for £115 then, on 20 February 1910, he escorted Ethel Le Neve to a ball for the Music Hall Ladies benevolent fund. Ethel was noticeably wearing a broach known to belong to Belle. On 12 March, Ethel moved in to 39 Hilltop Crescent, but Harvey told his landlord shortly after that he'd be moving out.

Harvey told Clara Martinetti that Belle was seriously ill and not expected to live. On 24 March, Clara received a telegram telling her that Belle had died. Harvey then took a trip with Ethel to Dieppe, France. While Harvey and Ethel were in France, Belle's friends discussed what had happened. Ethel continued to be seen wearing Belle's furs and jewels.

A friend of Belle's, John Nash, then paid a visit to America but was unable to find anything. John Nash and his wife spoke to Scotland Yard and, on 8 July, Chief Inspector Walter Dew spoke to Harvey, who explained that the story of his wife's death was a lie concocted to avoid the scandal of what he believed was Belle's running off with Bruce Miller. Dew obtained a search warrant for the Hilltop Crescent house but found nothing. Dew began to believe Harvey who might well have escaped justice, but instead he panicked.

He and Ethel took a boat to Antwerp, Belgium.

Walter Dew returned to the Crippen house to check some dates and found the house unoccupied. Dew became suspicious and put out a warrant. Authorities broadcasted the descriptions of Crippen and Le Neve. Dew returned to the house on 13 July where he found the remains of Belle buried in lime in the coal cellar.

This was the first murder case for the medical examiner, Sir Bernard Spilsbury. From his notes:

> Human remains found 13 July … Medical organs of chest and abdomen removed in one mass. Four large pieces of skin and muscle, one from lower abdomen with old operation scar four inches long—broader at lower end. Impossible to identify sex. Hyoscine found 2.7 grains. Hair in Hinde's curler—roots present. Hair 6 inches long. Man's pyjama jacket label reads Jones Bros., Holloway, and odd pair of pyjama trousers.

There was no head, all the limbs were missing and there were no bones, except for what appeared to be part of a human thigh. The remains were identified as Belle's from an operation scar present on a piece of skin. Hyoscine is a toxic alkaloid now used in small quantities for travel sickness. At the time it was thought to reduce sexual desire. Harvey claimed that he had given it to Belle for this reason.

One week before Harvey's trial what was left of Belle was reburied in Finchley Cemetery. The rest of her was never found. Harvey had burned her bones in the oven, dissolved her organs in acid in the bathtub and had put her head in a handbag, which he threw overboard while on the trip to Dieppe.

The papers were getting wind of the story on 20 July, when Harvey and Ethel boarded the *SS Montrose* from Antwerp to Canada. Ethel was poorly disguised as a boy. The *Montrose's* Captain, Henry Kendall, became suspicious when he observed that 'Mr. Robinson' was rather too affectionate with his 'son'. Having heard that Harvey had false teeth the Captain told him a joke. When Harvey laughed the Captain noticed his suspect's teeth were loose. Kendall radioed London on 22 July and Inspector Dew boarded a faster ship, the *SS Laurentic*. Dew arrested Harvey and Ethel on 31 July, as they alighted the *Montrose*.

★★★

They were tried *separately*. The trial at the Old Bailey lasted five days from 18–22 October 1919. Clara Martinetti and Bruce Miller were among the witnesses for the prosecution.

On the basis of the examination of the remains and the clothing found with them, the jury took all of 27 minutes to find Crippen guilty. Ethel Le Neve was found not guilty as an accessory at her trial, four days later.

On Wednesday, 23 November 1910, at Pentonville Prison in London, John Ellis, Harvey Crippen's hangman, noted that Crippen smiled as he walked towards him. He also noted that Crippen was 5ft 4ins (1.6m) tall and weighed 136lb (62kg) so Ellis gave him a drop of 7ft 9ins (2.4m). Crippen requested that a photograph of Ethel be buried with him. The request was granted.

Ellis later published his memoirs: *Diary of a Hangman*. He committed suicide in 1932.

German air raids destroyed 39 Hilltop Crescent during WWII.

On the dark and foggy morning of Harvey's execution Ethel sailed for New York as a 'Miss Allen'. She lived in Toronto under the name Ethel Harvey. During WWI she returned to London and later married an accountant, Stanley Smith. She died an 84-year-old grandmother in 1967.

1936

Cruelty Unlimited: Albert Fish

When you look at the history of crime, criminals, mass murderers and serial killers, you'd be hard-pressed to decide which one was the worst. The man who would later be known as the 'Moon Maniac', the 'Gray Man' and the 'Brooklyn Vampire' would certainly be way up there on any short-list for the title of 'Greatest Monster of the 20th Century.' It wasn't just that Albert Fish raped, tortured, mutilated and ate little children. He wrote to the parents afterwards 'explaining' what he'd done. It wasn't enough for Fish to be physically sadistic; he had to be psychologically sadistic as well.

The son of riverboat Captain Randal Fish, Hamilton Fish was born on 19 May 1870, in Washington DC. When his father died, on 15 October 1875, Hamilton Fish's mother placed him in St John's orphanage, where he spent the next four years being frequently and savagely whipped and beaten. This was probably not the best of upbringings for someone who had come from a long line of mentally ill people. In his book, *The Show of Violence,* Dr Frederic Wertham later wrote: 'One paternal uncle suffered from a religious psychosis and died in a state hospital. A half brother also died in a state hospital. A younger brother was feeble-minded and died of hydrocephalus. His mother was held to be "very queer" and was said to hear and see things. A paternal aunt was considered "completely crazy." A brother suffered from chronic alcoholism. A sister had some sort of "mental affliction".

Constantly teased for being called 'Hamilton', he took the name Albert instead.

In 1898 he married a 19-year-old woman. Throughout his marriage Fish was frequently in trouble with the police and was jailed for grand larceny in 1903. He and his wife had six children together before she left him and the children for another man in 1917. As far as anyone knows Fish never laid a finger on his own children and was an excellent father to them and his stepchildren from three subsequent marriages. That's if you don't count the bizarre games where the children would beat him with a hairbrush or the times he would show them how he stuck pins under his own fingernails.

Out of jail, a painter by profession, Fish spent years drifting throughout America, torturing and molesting children from poor black families. In the racist climate of the times there was little his victims could do about him.

July 1924, Staten Island

Fish unsuccessfully attempted to kidnap an eight-year-old girl. Years later, when Fish was in jail, the girl identified Fish as the 'Gray Man'. Three days later, Fish was more successful and kidnapped eight-year-old Francis McDonnell. In the woods near Charlton Woods, Fish tore off Francis' clothes, beat him savagely and strangled him with his suspenders.

11 February 1927, New York

Fish kidnapped four-year-old Billy Gaffney. He later confessed:

> 'I brought him to the Riker Ave dumps. There is a house that stands alone, not far from where I took him. I took the boy there, stripped him naked, tied his hands and feet and gagged him with a piece of dirty rag I picked out of the dump. Then I burned his clothes. Threw his shoes in the dump. Then I walked back and took the trolley to 59 St. at 2 am and walked from there home.

'Next day about 2 pm, I took tools, a good heavy cat-of-nine tails; home made, short handle. Cut one of my belts in half, slit these halves in six strips about 8 inches long (20cm). I whipped his bare behind till the blood ran from his legs. I cut off his ears and nose, slit his mouth from ear to ear, gouged out his eyes. He was dead then. I stuck the knife in his belly and held my mouth to his body and drank his blood.

'I picked up four old potato sacks and gathered a pile of stones. Then I cut him up. I had a grip with me. I put his nose, ears and a few slices of his belly in the grip. Then I cut him through the middle of his body—just below the belly button—then through his legs about two inches below his behind. I put this in my grip with a lot of paper. I cut off the head, feet, arms, hands and the legs below the knee. This I put in sacks weighted with stones, tied the ends and threw them into the pools of slimy water you will see all along the road going to North Beach.

'I came home with my meat. I had the front of his body I liked best. His monkey and pee wees and a nice, little fat behind to roast in the oven and eat. I made a stew out of his ears, nose, pieces of his face and belly. I put onions, carrots, turnips, celery, salt and pepper. It was good.

'Then I split the cheeks of his behind open, cut off his monkey and pee wees and washed them first. I put strips of bacon on each cheek of his behind and put them in the oven. Then I picked four onions and when the meat had roasted about 1/4 hour, I poured about a pint of water over it for gravy and put in the onions. At frequent intervals I basted his behind with a wooden spoon. So the meat would be nice and juicy.

'In about two hours, it was nice and brown, cooked through. I never ate any roast turkey that tasted half as good as his sweet, fat little behind did. I ate every bit of the meat in about four days. His little monkey was a sweet as a nut, but his pee-wees I could not chew. Threw them in the toilet.'

FRIDAY 25 MAY 1928

17-year-old Edward Budd placed a classified ad in the Sunday edition of the *New York World* seeking employment in the country. On Monday 28 May, a thin, frail-looking, elderly man visited the Budd family at their tenement at 406 West 15th St in Manhattan. He claimed to be a farmer from Farmingdale, Long Island called Frank Howard. 'Frank' needed a young man to work on his farm and told that the Budds that their son fit the bill, he would even hire Willie, Edwards's best friend. Although Fish was only 155cm tall and weighed 60kg he was confident that he could overpower the young men. On Saturday 2 June, the Budds received a note from 'Frank' saying he would see them in the morning. Fish was busy buying a cleaver, a saw and a butcher's knife. On Sunday 3 June, Howard revisited the Budds, bringing strawberries and pot cheese from his 'farm'.

When he saw Albert and Delia Budd's 10-year-old daughter, Grace, however, he decided he wanted to kill her instead. With the talent for engendering trust that child molesters often inspire, he convinced the Budd's to allow Grace to accompany him to his niece's party at his sister's home at Columbus and 137th St that evening. The address didn't exist. The Budds never saw their daughter again.

More than 20 detectives were assigned to the case.

Although police in New York arrested Fish six times over the next few years—on charges ranging from petty larceny to vagrancy—they never connected him to Grace Budd and all their efforts in that investigation came to nothing.

In the winter of 1930 Fish was arrested for writing obscene letters. He spent 30 days in the psychiatric ward at Bellevue Hospital in New York, but was released when he was judged to be 'harmless.'

1932

Fish was painting a house in Far Rockaway and took time out to murder 15-year-old Mary O'Connor.

NOVEMBER 1934

Six years after Grace's kidnapping, the Budds received a letter. Delia Budd was illiterate and couldn't read it. Edward, now 23, did and immediately ran to the police.

> 'My dear Mrs Budd,
> In 1894 a friend of mine shipped as a deck hand on the steamer *Tacoma*, Captain John Davis. They sailed from San Francisco for Hong Kong, China. On arriving there he and two others went ashore and got drunk. When they returned the boat was gone.
>
> At that time there was famine in China. Meat of any kind was from $1 to $3 a pound. So great was the suffering among the very poor that all children under 12 were sold for food in order to keep others from starving. A boy or girl under 14 was not safe in the street. You could go in any shop and ask for steak, chops or stew meat. Part of the naked body of a boy or girl would be brought out and just what you wanted cut from it. A boy or girls behind which is the sweetest part of the body and sold as veal cutlet brought the highest price.
>
> John stayed there so long he acquired a taste for human flesh. On his return to New York he stole two boys one seven, one 11. Took them to his home, stripped them naked, tied them in a closet. Then burned everything they had on. Several times every day and night he spanked them—tortured them—to make their meat good and tender.
>
> First he killed the 11-year-old boy, because he had the fattest ass and of course the most meat on it. Every part of his body was cooked and eaten except the head, bones and guts. He was roasted in the oven (all of his ass), boiled, broiled, fried and stewed. The little boy was next, went the same way. At that time, I was living at 409 E 100 St. near-right side. He told me so often how good human flesh was I made up my mind to taste it.
>
> On Sunday June the 3, 1928 I called on you at 406 W 15 St. Brought you pot cheese—strawberries. We had lunch. Grace sat in my lap and kissed me. I made up my mind to eat her.

> On the pretence of taking her to a party, you said "Yes" she could go. I took her to an empty house in Westchester I had already picked out. When we arrived, I told her to remain outside. She picked wildflowers. I went upstairs and stripped all my clothes off. I knew if I did not I would get her blood on them.
>
> When all was ready, I went to the window and called her. Then I hid in a closet until she was in the room. When she saw me all naked she began to cry and tried to run down the stairs. I grabbed her and she said she would tell her mamma.
>
> First I stripped her naked. How she did kick, bite and scratch. I choked her to death, then cut her in small pieces so I could take my meat to my rooms. Cook and eat it. How sweet and tender her little ass was roasted in the oven. It took me nine days to eat her entire body. I did not fuck her, tho' I could of had I wished. She died a virgin.'

***

The letter was no fake.

The details of the meeting, six years earlier, were too accurate and the handwriting identical to the note that the Budds had received on 2 June, six years before. Police traced the stationary that the note had been written on. A young chauffeur, Lee Sicowski admitted that he'd taken paper and envelopes from the New York Private Chauffeurs Benevolent Association and left it in his old boarding house at 200 E 52nd St. The landlady there matched the description of 'Frank Howard' to her former tenant Albert Fish, who had stayed in Sicowski's old room.

On 13 December 1934 Fish came to pick up a letter that his son had sent him to his former address. Detective William F King arrested him on the spot and was shocked when Fish attacked him with a razor. Fish was no match for King who was no vulnerable child and he quickly overpowered the older man. 'I've got you now,' he said.

Fish began a long and incredibly detailed confession. He spoke of taking Grace Budd by train to an abandoned two-storey house, called Wisteria Cottage, in the woods near the village of Worthington in

Westchester. He talked about his sexual arousal when he strangled her, how he chopped off her head, caught her blood in an old paint bucket, cut her body in two and wrapped up her choicest body parts in newspaper to take with him.

He would later admit to quivering with excitement as Grace's body parts sat on his lap as the train took him back to New York. When police asked him why he killed and why he wrote letters he said, simply, 'You know, I never could account for it … I just had a mania for writing.' Later that night, however, when Assistant District Attorney, P Francis Marro, interrogated him, Fish spoke of 'a sort of blood thirst' followed by tremendous sorrow, 'I would have given my life within a half-hour after I'd done it to restore it to her.'

***

Fish was an eclectic consumer. He ate not only his victim's flesh, but drank their blood, their urine and ate their excrement.

Police were eventually able to link Fish to the murder of 15 children and the molestation and mutilation of about a hundred others.

Fish was a sadomasochist and the pain and injury that he inflicted on himself was almost as bizarre as that which he inflicted on his victims. He would regularly flagellate himself with nail-studded paddles. Frederic Wertham wrote: 'He took bits of cotton, saturated them with alcohol, inserted them into his rectum and set fire to them. He also did that with his child victims.' Fish also described his practice of inserting a thorny stem of a rose into his penis, then eating the stem afterwards.

When doctors X-rayed him they found at least 29 needles that Fish had pushed into himself over the years and could not get out.

Fish expressed surprise that none of his children visited him in jail. Shortly after Fish's arrest, Albert Fish Junior gave a newspaper interview:

> 'That old skunk. I always knew that he would get caught for something like this … I've never wanted anything to do with him and I'll not lift a hand to help him.'

Fish's trial opened on 11 March 1935. He tried pleading insanity, telling the court that God told him to kill children: 'What I did must have been right or an angel would have stopped me, just as an angel stopped Abraham in the Bible.'

Psychiatrists for the prosecution testified that a man could be a coprophile, a urophile, a paedophile, a necrophile and a religiously delusional sadomasochist without necessarily being insane. In one memorable moment during the trial, prosecutor Chief Assistant District Attorney, Elbert F Gallagher, held up Grace Budd's skull for the jury to see.

After 10 days of trial and four hours of deliberation, the jury found Fish sane and guilty of the murder of Grace Budd. The judge pronounced the death sentence: Fish thanked him for it.

Fish's last meal was steak. On 16 January 1936, at 11:09 pm, 65-year-old Albert Fish became the oldest man ever executed at Sing Sing prison. True to form he had eagerly anticipated his execution:

'Going to the electric chair will be the supreme thrill of my life ... the only thrill I have not tried.'

He even helped the guards strap him to the chair. A daily news reporter wrote that Fish's '... watery eyes gleamed at the thought of being burned by a heat more intense that the flames with which he often seared his flesh to gratify his lust'.

***

There is no truth to the rumour that Fish had to be electrocuted twice because the first electrocution short-circuited on account of the needles Fish had in his body.

In the hours before his death Fish wrote a final statement, the contents of which have not been revealed. His defence attorney, James Dempsey, said: 'I will never show it to anyone, it was the most filthy string of obscenities that I have ever read.'

A couple of days after the execution, Dempsey received a letter from Fish, thanking him for his efforts on his behalf.

Near the end of the letter Fish wrote: 'I do not wish to die, God has more work for me to do.'

1950–1953

10 Rillington Place: Timothy Evans and John Christie

There's a sense of darkness about 10 Rillington Place. The poor, closed-in, musky terrace house in a dingy industrial suburb of London is as much a character as the people who lived in it. It's not a black darkness though. It's grey: as if the evil there was somehow second-rate. The sheer, depressing mediocrity of the place seems a fitting backdrop to the bizarre bond that held two men together and made 10 Rillington Place a house that would hold not one, but two murderers—or was it only one after all?

John Reginald Halliday Christie was born on 8 April 1899, just outside Halifax, Yorkshire in England. By all accounts he was a bright child, but his relationships with women were, to say the least, problematical. His mother was stiflingly overprotective and his four older sisters bullied him. His first sexual experience was a disaster that turned into a fiasco when the girl involved started telling everybody how hopeless he was. He had to suffer nicknames like 'Can't make it Christie' and 'Reggie-No-Dick.'

His relationships with men weren't much better. His father was a strict disciplinarian who beat his children regularly. Christie later recalled that, when he was eight years old, he experienced 'fascination and pleasure' looking at the corpse of his grandfather, of whom he had always been afraid. It is possible that at this young age, John Christie learned to associate the death of people he feared and hated with a sense of freedom, liberation and empowerment.

He served in World War I and suffered a gas injury in France in 1918. The damage to his throat left him 'quietly spoken' for the rest of his life, which suited his pale, bespectacled, balding, generally non-descript appearance. Christie was given to using hypochondria to gain sympathy. Back in Halifax on 10 May 1920, he married dowdy Ethel Simpson Waddington, one of six women, perhaps seven, who he would later murder.

Christie's criminal career started off small: stealing postal orders while working as a postman, for which he served three months in prison in 1921. His sporadic work history, sexual neglect of his wife and constant visits to prostitutes didn't help his marriage and in 1924 Ethel went to live with relatives in Sheffield. In 1929 he was living with and off a prostitute. His ingratitude knew no bounds and one day, during an argument, he struck her on the head with a cricket bat. The court gave him six months hard labour for the assault and in 1933 another jury sentenced him to three months for stealing a car from a priest. While in jail he asked Ethel to come back to him. Amazingly, and although they had been separated for 10 years, she agreed.

In 1938, the Christies moved in to 10 Rillington Place, Notting Hill, North Kensington in London. The Christies lived on the ground floor. Retired railway worker Charles Kitchener lived on the first floor and the second floor was unoccupied at the time that the couple moved in.

In 1939 World War II began and the London police force started recruiting volunteer Special Constables for the War Reserve Police. Christie applied. No one looked too closely into his past and they gave him the job. He also began an affair with a woman whose husband was serving overseas. The affair ended abruptly when the husband returned, found Christie in bed with his wife and promptly gave Christie a beating.

In 1943, while his wife was back with her relatives in Sheffield, Christie began an affair with 21-year-old Austrian student nurse, munitions factory worker and part-time prostitute, Ruth Margarete Fuerst. On 24 August 1943, he strangled Ruth with a rope while having sex with her. As he pulled away from her she released urine and excrement, suggesting that she was dead before he was finished. Later Christie would write:

'I remember as I gazed down at the still form of my first victim, experiencing a strange, peaceful thrill.' He wrapped the body in her coat and hid it under the floorboards of the ground floor, front room. His wife and her brother arrived later that evening. The next day, after she had gone to work and her brother had left, he moved Ruth's body into the washhouse, dug a grave in the garden and buried her at 10 o'clock that night. He burned her clothing in the backyard dustbin.

In early 1944 Christie left the Special Constables to work in an electrical factory. There he met 31-year-old canteen worker, Muriel Amelia Eady. Muriel suffered persistent catarrh and, while Ethel Christie was again in Sheffield, Christie suggested that she visit him. He claimed to have a device that would 'cure' Muriel's chronic inflammation of her mucous membranes. Christie's device contained Friars Balsam, an alcoholic solution of benzoin, styrax, tolu balsam and aloes, usually used to treat blocked sinuses. Unknown to Muriel, Christie had attached a hose to his device through which he pumped house gas. Unlike the natural gas used in modern houses, the industrially-produced gas at the time could rapidly render someone unconscious, as it did to Muriel this time. While she was passing out Christie had sex with her while strangling her. He then put her body in the washhouse and buried it in the garden afterwards.

At the end of the war Christie returned to work at the post office. He waited four years before he killed again.

Timothy John Evans was born in Wales in 1924. With a measured IQ of only 68, the mentally backward, short, slight, sickly and illiterate van driver married 18-year-old Beryl Thorley in 1947. They lived with Evans' mother and his sisters in a house not far from the Christies. Then Beryl became pregnant and they needed to find a place on their own.

During Easter 1948 the couple moved to 10 Rillington Place. Baby Geraldine was born in October 1948. By mid-1949, Beryl was pregnant again. Realising that there was no way they could afford another child she was desperate for an abortion: a fact that she frequently the told the Christies.

In October 1949 Christie complained about a blocked drain. Workers arrived on 31 October and carried out their work over the next 15 days. The first floor lodger, Charles Kitchener, was in hospital. During those crucial two weeks the Christies were alone in the house with the Evans family.

On 20 November 1949, Timothy Evans walked into the police station in Merthyr Tidfyl in Wales and confessed to killing his 20-year-old wife. The accounts of Evans' confessions and Christie's confessions are varied and contradictory and the truth of what happened in early November 1949 will probably never be known for certain.

Evan's first story was that on 7 November he gave Beryl a bottle of pills to induce an abortion, but the next day he found his wife dead at home and hid her body in a drain outside 10 Rillington Place. Notting Hill Police investigated the drain and discovered that it took four men to lift the drain cover. When they did, there was nothing there. Evans was lying. Caught out, he now told a different story. He said that John Christie had offered to help arrange an abortion for Beryl, but when he (Evans) came home from work his wife was dead, bleeding from the mouth, nose and 'the bottom part.' Christie told him, 'It's bad news; it didn't work,' and that they had to hide the body or they would both go to jail.

On their second visit to Rillington Place the police searched the Evans' apartment and found newspaper clippings from the Stanley Setty torso murder case. While superficially incriminating, it didn't seem to occur to police that there was something odd about an illiterate man collecting newspaper clippings.

In another example of incompetence, police also didn't notice that Muriel Eady's thighbone had worked its way to the surface and Christie was using it to prop up the garden fence.

Christie's dog had also dug up her skull. Eventually Christie simply took it to a bombed house at 133 St Mark's Road, where authorities later assumed it to belong to an unknown blitz victim.

Extradited to London, Evans changed his story again. This time he claimed that he strangled his wife on 8 November and then strangled his daughter on 10 November. In England at the time the standard legal procedure was to proceed for one murder only, so he was charged with the murder of Geraldine. When police questioned Christie he dismissed Evans' account as 'ludicrous'. They believed him.

On 2 December the police returned to Rillington Place and found the decaying bodies of Beryl and Geraldine wrapped in a green tablecloth and hidden behind some wood in the outhouse. Both mother and daughter had been strangled. In Beryl's case a tie was so tightly wrapped around her neck that it had to be cut out in order to remove it.

Evans' trial was only three days long, 11–13 January 1950. At the trial he retracted his confession and blamed Christie. Christie, as a witness for the prosecution, presented himself as a frail victim who had never done anything but to try help the Evans. He completely denied Evans' accusations. The jury, the prosecution and even the defence chose to believe that Evans was guilty and failed to examine discrepancies in the various versions of events. Eventually, after only 40 minutes of deliberation, the jury found Evans guilty of the murder of 14-month-old Geraldine. He was hanged at Pentonville prison, on 9 March 1950. He was 25 years old.

The trial had uncovered Christie's past and he lost his job at the post office. Over the next few years Christie's indolence and hypochondria became worse, Ethel was suffering from chronic arthritis and rheumatism and their marriage deteriorated further.

The last day anyone saw 55-year-old Ethel Christie alive was 12 December 1952. Early on 14 December Christie strangled his wife with a stocking. The post-mortem later revealed that he did not have sex with her. He left the body on the bed for three days before he decided to wrapped it in blankets and hide it under the floorboards of the front room. He told her relatives in Sheffield that Ethel was sick and he told his neighbours that Ethel was in Sheffield. For the next few months, he sold all his furniture and lived on Ethel's savings.

In mid-January 1953 Christie rigged up a chair at his house with a gas tube, held closed with a clip. He met up with 26-year-old Paddington prostitute, Kathleen Maloney, got her very drunk and then invited her home with him. While she sat in the chair Christie removed the clip. As she fell into unconsciousness, Christie strangled her with a rope. The next morning, while the corpse was still sitting in the chair, Christie made tea. He then wrapped her body in a blanket, put a pillowcase over her head and hid her body in the alcove behind the washhouse.

On 19 January 1953 Christie successfully used the inhalant device scam again on another woman, 25-year-old, 25-weeks-pregnant prostitute, Rita Nelson. Christie hid her body next to that of Maloney.

Hectorina McLennan, 26, was living with an unemployed lorry driver called Baker when Christie invited her to see him in early March 1953 on the pretext of seeing a flat. When McLennan failed to show up for a meeting with Baker, the man visited Christie. He didn't find her, but he did notice a bad smell from near the rear of the house.

On 13 March, with no money and no job, Christie successfully sublet his rooms to a Mr and Mrs Reilly, taking three month's rent in advance. The day after the Reillys moved in the Rillington Place landlord, Charles Brown, evicted them, saying that Christie had had no right to sublet his rooms. The Reillys were glad to go anyway: the place smelled terrible.

On 24 March, Charles Brown allowed a new tenant, Beresford Brown, to use the Christies' former kitchen. While trying to mount wall brackets he ripped off a loose piece of wallpaper and found the alcove behind the washhouse. He saw the naked back of a woman's body.

The next day the newspapers were full of reports of the bodies of the six women that the police had found there: the corpses of McLennan, Maloney and Nelson in the alcove, the remains of Fuerst and Eady in the garden and that of Ethel Christie under the floorboards in the front room.

Christie had run out of money and had been wandering aimlessly about London for 10 days when, on 31 March, Police Constable Tom Ledger spotted Christie on the Putney embankment of the Thames and arrested him. He confessed to killing the six women, but always claimed that the three prostitutes had approached him and he that had to kill them after they forced themselves upon him. He claimed that he had killed the other three women because they were suffering from depression and he wanted to 'put them out of their misery'.

Probably in an attempt to escape with an insanity plea, Christie confessed to killing Beryl Evans too. 'The more the merrier', he said, but he did not confess to killing Geraldine Evans. The psychiatrists who examined Christie in Brixton prison, described him as 'nauseating' and 'snivelling'.

His trial lasted three days from 22 June. The jury rejected his insanity plea and after 85 minutes returned a verdict of guilty of murder. Christie did not appeal. He was hanged at Pentonville Prison on 15 July 1953.

In light of Christie's confession the Evans' case was reopened. The Henderson Report published its findings on the day of Christie's execution. It concluded that Evans had killed his wife and daughter. In 1965 the subsequent Brabin inquiry determined that although Evans probably killed his wife, Christie had probably killed Geraldine. Since Evans had been convicted for Geraldine's murder he was granted a posthumous pardon in 1966. His was the first pardon to be granted in the 20th century.

***

Some years after the murders Rillington Place was renamed Ruston Close. The movie, *10 Rillington Place*, was filmed in 1970 at number 8. It had identical dimensions to the original house and gave the viewer an accurate idea of the cramped, dark and dingy atmosphere of the three-storey Victorian terrace. Ruston Close was demolished in 1971 and the whole area redeveloped. The closest equivalent street now is Bartle Road. The site of the washhouse and the hidden alcove where five of the bodies were found is to the left of steps leading to the park next to St Andrew's Square, between Bartle Road and Lancaster Road.

1955

Crime of Passion: Ruth Ellis

One woman. One man. One murder. Not usually the stuff that attracts that much attention. But there must have been something about the time. Only a couple of years before Marilyn Monroe had achieved stardom in the thriller Niagara, *in which a beautiful young woman plots to kill her husband. Maybe the parallels were just too good to resist. England would have its own real-life platinum-blonde killer and an otherwise pathetic story would suddenly catapult into the realm of myth.*

The 16th and last woman to be hanged in Britain during the 20th century started life in 1926 as Ruth Hornby, in Rhyl, North Wales. Her father, a cellist, had changed his name for professional reasons, but by 1933 Arthur Neilson's career was over and he became a maudlin, violent drunk who apparently sexually abused both Ruth and her older sister Muriel (Muriel has since revealed that she bore Arthur's child when she was 18). Arthur provided a role model for the future men in Ruth's life.

Ruth moved to London in 1941 and started to dye her hair blonde, which gave the society of the time the impression that she was a cheap tart, an impression that didn't help later at her trial. She fell pregnant to a serviceman named Clare who soon returned to his wife and three children in Canada. Ruth Hornby never saw Clare again, but she gave birth to their son. She named the child after his father's surname and used her own father's original name. Clare Andrea Neilson was born on 15 September 1945.

Ruth started working as a nude model for a camera club for £1 per hour to support herself and her baby. While modelling she met the ugly but affable club owner, Morrie Conley, who offered her work as a hostess at his Court Club at 58 Duke Street for £5 per week, plus commissions. Over the next nine years Morrie promoted Ruth to the management of several of his 'establishments'. He also used and abused her when he was drunk. Ruth stayed because the lifestyle of fine clothes and free drinks suited her. Working with Conley also gave Ruth the opportunity to mingle with a 'better class of men'. Ruth made money and helped support her parents and sister Muriel, who brought up Ruth's son, 'Andy'. Early in 1950 she became pregnant by one of her clients. She had an abortion and was drinking more and more heavily when she met a dentist, George Johnson Ellis. She married him in a fit of infatuation. The relationship, like all of Ruth's relationships with men, was a disaster. George, a divorced father of two sons was 16 years older than Ruth. He was a musician and a drunk—just like Ruth's father. Ruth eventually became violently and irrationally obsessed with the idea the George was cheating on her, to the point where Dr TP Rees, the psychiatrist treating George for alcoholism, started prescribing drugs for Ruth too. By the time that Ruth split up with George in 1951, she was pregnant with their daughter, Georgina, who was born later that year. Ironically, it was George who filed the petition to divorce Ruth, on the grounds of cruelty.

With two children to support and desperate for money, Ruth continued to work in Morrie Conley's clubs. At one of them, Carroll's, she first encountered David Blakely, who behaved so badly that Ruth asked a friend: 'Who is that pompous little ass?'

David Blakely was a public school-educated, racing car groupie and champion wannabe. Through his stepfather's influence he worked as a management trainee and later at Silicone Pistons, but his stepfather and mother frequently had to 'supplement' his income so that David could support his racing habit. Racer Cliff Davis said of David:

> 'He liked his booze … he wasn't averse to poncing it and he certainly ponced off Ruth. David was a good-looking, supercilious shit, but you couldn't help liking him. I knew he used to knock her around … theirs was a love-hate relationship, as unstable as a stick of dynamite.'

That relationship began almost immediately after Ruth became manager of Morrie's Little Club, in Knightsbridge. Somehow they connected and moved in together—in spite of their earlier encounter; in spite of the fact that Ruth was still Mrs Ellis at the time and in spite of the fact that David was engaged to Linda Dawson, the daughter of a wealthy manufacturer from Huddlesfield.

David treated Ruth like garbage and was ashamed of her despite his attraction to her. He once forced her to wait in a car rather than introduce her to his mother.

Then, on 17 June 1954, Ruth began an affair with Desmond Edward Cusson in retaliation for David's failure to return home on time from racing in Le Mans. Desmond fell totally in love with Ruth, but couldn't compete with the younger, more dashing and better looking David. At this time George Ellis reappeared on the scene, demanding that Ruth finalise their divorce. Ruth resisted in order to continue receiving George's maintenance payments. David spent increasing amounts of time building a racing car, *The Emperor* with a friend, Anthony 'Ant' Findlater, the husband of Carole, a former lover of David's. David had also run up an enormous bar tab at the Little Club. When the club stopped making money Morrie either sacked Ruth or she quit.

Out of work and out of money, she moved into Desmond Cusson's flat. Ruth played David and Desmond off each other. She explained her absences—when she was with David—to Desmond by telling him she was visiting her daughter, who had been adopted out to the north of England. She told David that, although she was living with Desmond, she wasn't sleeping with him. David continued to call Ruth a tart, while Ruth accused David of continuing his affair with Carole Findlater. In late 1954 David became involved with an older married woman and Ruth threatened to have some of her gangster friends do something about it. In the midst of frequent brawls and reconciliations, Ruth forced

Desmond to drive her around in order to check up on David. Finally David and Ruth rented a bedsit at 44 Egerton Gardens under the name of Mr and Mrs Ellis.

In late March Ruth discovered she was pregnant again, father unknown. David, in a fury, hit Ruth in the abdomen and she lost the baby. Then on 2 April 1955, *The Emperor* blew up in a practice lap of a race. David blamed Ruth, calling her a jinx.

On Friday, 8 April, David said he was going to visit Ant Findlater. When he didn't return that evening Ruth started calling the Findlater's. Ant assured her that David wasn't there, but Ruth 'knew' he was and that the Findlaters were 'laughing behind her back'. She rang them so often that the Findlaters took the phone off the hook.

The now hysterical Ruth made Desmond drive her to the Findlaters'. When they arrived she started banging doors, smashing windows and wrecking David's car. The police were called and eventually Desmond persuaded Ruth to leave.

David was indeed at the Findlater's the whole time, claiming that he was trying to escape from Ruth. That Saturday morning Ruth returned in time to see David and Ant depart in David's car. In twenty-four hours Ruth made Desmond drive her to the Findlater's four times and made several more attempts to speak to them on the phone.

Finally, after days without sleep, tanked to the gills on Pernod and Dr Rees's drugs, Ruth once again made her long-suffering patsy Desmond drive her to the Findlater's. When she arrived she saw that David's car was gone. She guessed, correctly, that David would be at the Magdala Tavern in nearby South Hill Park. She made Desmond drive her there. When they drove up there was David's car.

She kissed Desmond and said 'Thank you for being there when I needed you, and looking after me and Andy, and being patient and kind and everything ...'

Desmond then drove off and Ruth waited across the road. David and a friend, Chris Gunnell, emerged from the Magdala. Ruth called out to David: he ignored her. Ruth fired a shot that missed completely. The next four shots did hit David, blasting through his windpipe, aorta, intestines and liver. Ruth saved the last bullet for herself, but the gun jammed.

Stunned, Ruth fired the gun into a paving stone. It ricocheted and hit a bystander, Mrs Gladys Yule, on the thumb before shattering and leaving marks on the Magdala Tavern.

When it was over an off-duty policeman, Alan Thompson, arrested her.

At her trial on the 20th and 21st of June 1955, Ruth said: 'It is obvious that when I shot him that I intended to kill him.' The jury took 14 minutes to find her guilty of murder. Ruth did not appeal the conviction. She believed it was right that she die. She even wrote to David's mother, apologising for killing him.

On Wednesday 13 July she was hanged at Holloway jail. The hangman, Albert Pierrepoint, wrote to her mother to remark on how bravely she met her death. Ruth had no 'last words', according Pierrepoint, 'She never spoke'. She was buried on the grounds of Holloway and, when Holloway was demolished, her son, Andy, successfully applied to have her reburied at St Mary's Parish Church under the name Ruth Hornby.

The Findlaters divorced in 1956. Ant remarried and moved to France.

The public furore over Ruth's case led to the Homicide Act 1957 that redefined those crimes that were classed as 'capital' and also introduced the defence of diminished responsibility.

After Ruth's death, her mother, Bertha Hornby, became mentally deranged and died in a psychiatric hospital, a few years after Ruth's father's death. In 1958 George Ellis hanged himself in a room in Le Chalet Hotel, in Corbiere, Jersey.

Desmond always denied helping Ruth, but some years later her son, Andy, said that he saw Desmond showing Ruth how to use the .38 Smith and Wesson with which she shot David.

Desmond emigrated to Australia in 1964 and, after numerous business failures, ended up in Perth. British television producer Peter Williams interviewed him in June 1977. Desmond seemed wistful and nostalgic about the whole affair, remarking that Ruth had achieved her ambition to be a star. Desmond died in Perth on 8 May 1991 of pneumonia aggravated by alcoholism.

Desmond paid for Andy's education but had never contacted him.

Andy's childhood had been one long, unstable round of pass-the-buck from one carer to another and he grew to be an unbalanced and confused adult. In 1980, at the age of 36, he took a mixture of drugs and alcohol and killed himself in his flat in Euston, North London.

A movie of Ruth's story, *Dance with a Stranger*, was made in 1985.

In 2002 Ruth's sister, Muriel Jakubait, now of Woking, Surry and Ruth's daughter, Georgie, began a process with the Criminal Cases Review Commission to have Ruth's case reheard. This resulted in an appeal in September 2003, which confirmed that Ruth was guilty of murder under the law, as it existed at the time.

Georgie was adopted out and didn't learn her true identity until she found newspaper clippings at the age of eight. In 1995 she published *Ruth Ellis, My Mother.* She died from cancer, aged 50, in December 2001.

Muriel published a book in July 2005 called *Ruth Ellis: My Sister's Secret Life,* in which she offers an account of Ruth in which she was 'set up' for a killing she really didn't commit.

'It's no accident my sister carried the can. That murder was organised like a military exercise by experts. Ruth was hand picked. And she shielded those people who'd picked her ... the ones who promised her she wouldn't die'.

The Emperor is on display at the Westridge Museum on The Isle of Wight.

On the outside of the Magdala, at 2a South Hill Park, NW3 5BB, you can still see the damage caused by the bullet that ricocheted from Gladys Yule's thumb.

1967

The Last Australians

Almost the whole Australian continent was once a prison, at least from a European perspective. The figures are a little contradictory. An article posted on the Australian Institute of Criminology website even says that as many as 80 convicts per year were executed in the 1800s (total in excess of 8000), yet also shows a table that gives a total of only 1648 executions for the years between 1820 and 1899. It's therefore difficult to know exactly how many legally-sanctioned executions Australia has had. Hanging though, was almost universally the method of choice. 128 people were hanged in Australia during the 20th century.

The last executions in Australia were all hangings. In chronological order and state by state they were:

Queensland, 22 September 1913, Brisbane Gaol: Earnest Austin, rape and murder of a little girl.
New South Wales, 24 August 1939, Long Bay Gaol, Sydney: John Kelly, murder.
Tasmania, 14 February 1946, Hobart Gaol: Frederick Thompson, murder.
Northern Territory, 8 August 1952, Darwin Gaol: Jerry Coci and Jonus Nopoty, murder of a taxi driver.

Western Australia, 26 October, 1964, Fremantle Gaol: Eric Edgar Cooke, serial murderer.
South Australia, 24 November 1964, Adelaide Gaol: Glen Sabre Valance, murder of his employer and the rape of his employer's wife.
Victoria, 3 February 1967, Pentridge Prison, Melbourne: Ronald Ryan, murder of George Hodson, a prison warder.

Because of its low population, comparatively non-violent recent history and almost forty years with an abolitionist policy, Australia is relatively tame when it comes to Death Row, nevertheless, some individuals and events are worth special mention.

1951: JEAN LEE

Born Marjorie Jean Maude Wright on 10 December 1919 in Dubbo, the last woman to be hanged in Australia was the youngest of five. People remember her as a bright, popular and rebellious student, but when she left school she had a few dead-end jobs and married in 1938. In April 1939 she gave birth to her only child, daughter Jillian. Ten years later, in 1949, Lee's husband left her and—in a scenario reminiscent of Ruth Ellis—Jean gave her daughter to her mother to raise. Lee's mother eventually won outright custody. The legal wrangle over Jillian left Lee feeling betrayed and her life began to go further downhill. Eventually she met compulsive gambler and petty criminal Robert David Clayton. Lee became a prostitute and Clayton became her pimp. As in so many other cases, before and since, Lee became a woman in love with a man who felt free to use and abuse her.

Lee and Clayton started making money playing the 'Badger Game.' Lee would lure men into sexually compromising positions. Clayton would then 'suddenly' appear, playing the outraged husband. When threatened with blackmail, the would-be johns handed over money to stop their wives finding out. When they didn't fork over Clayton beat them up. It worked, mostly.

While serving time in prison Clayton met Norman Andrews and they became friends. Then, on the evening of 7 November 1949, Lee, Clayton and Andrews found another mark at Carlton's University Hotel. He was

SP bookie and boarding house owner, William 'Pop' Kent. Jean plied her charms and established that Kent was not only drunk, but probably had a stash of money at home. Lee persuaded Kent to take them to his boarding house in Dorritt Street, nearby. Once there, alone with Kent in his room, Lee tried to pick his pockets. Kent wasn't so drunk that he didn't notice and he started scuffling with Lee. Soon after Clayton and Andrews barged in. Clayton and Andrews tied Kent's thumbs behind his back with bootlaces and—for the next hour—they beat, kicked and tortured Kent to force him to tell them where he hid his money. When they ran out of patience they stabbed him repeatedly with a small knife. Finally, Clayton strangled him.

Neighbours heard Kent's screams and called the police, who soon traced the three to their hotel rooms, where they found their bloodstained clothing. Under questioning, Lee made a false confession to take the blame off her lover. 'No, they didn't do it, I did the lot,' she said, but soon the denials turned into pointing the blame at each other.

On 20 March 1950 the trial began. Six days later the jury took less than three hours to find Jean Lee, David Robert Clayton and Robert Andrews guilty of the murder of William 'Pop' Kent under the principle of common purpose. This made Lee guilty even though she had not actually strangled Kent. When Justice Gavan Duffy sentenced them to death, Clayton shouted abuse at the jury and Lee became hysterical, protesting her innocence.

At this point the case became highly political. On 23 June 1950 the Court of Criminal Appeal granted them a retrial on the grounds that their statements to the police had been improperly obtained. The High Court overturned the appeal and confirmed the convictions and death sentences. When Lee heard the decision she screamed, attacked her prison guard and started to throw herself against the walls of her cell. She had to be sedated. She became increasingly erratic, alternating between abusing her guards and pathetically begging for alcohol; see-sawing between hope and despair. 'I haven't enough strength in my hands to choke anyone. Bobby was stupid but the old man was trying to yell for help. None of us meant to kill him.' Her family, feeling disgraced, stopped visiting after the High Court ruling. In a move unique to Australian legal history the Victorian Government proceeded to schedule the executions, without waiting for a decision from the Privy Council.

Mass public protests continued throughout, particularly from women, but their protest came to nothing in the face of the men's expediency.

Lee angrily insisted on her innocence to the end. On the morning of her execution, 19 February 1951, a doctor had to sedate her and then resedate her.

The executioner 'Mr Jones' and his assistant walked into her cell in H-Division at Pentridge Gaol. They were hooded and wearing steel-rimmed executioner's goggles. Lee fainted. By now she was unconscious. 'Mr Jones' and his assistant carried Jean away. She was unable to stand up, so they put a chair on the gallows' trap door and seated Jean down. They had tied her hands together so that her arms rested in front of her body. They tied her feet together and put a hood over her head. They tied the chair to a rope. By law, Sheriff Willian Daly read the death warrant to an unconscious woman. The trap door opened and she and the chair fell together. She was hanged while the chair hung.

The government had executed her without waiting for the due process of appeal to the Privy Council, so … the hanging was illegal. She was the first woman to be hanged in Victoria since 'Baby Farmer' Frances Knorr in 1894 and only the second woman to hang in Australia in the 20th century. She was 31 years old.

Two hours later they hanged Robert David Clayton. The execution was botched. The Victorian Government pathologist estimated that he might have spent 15 minutes choking to death as he hanged from the rope.

In an interview on ABC radio on 29 April 2000, Poet Jordie Albiston spoke of Lee's hanging: 'I think it was the move of a fairly hysterical conservative government who was trying to recreate some order after the war and looking at women to return to the homes and keep the family stable.'

1964: ERIC EDGAR COOKE

The most notorious serial killer to be executed in Australia and the last man to be hanged in Western Australia, Eric Edgar Cooke terrorised the city of Perth in the 1960s. The half million people who lived there at the time still thought Perth was just a big country town. They felt that they knew their neighbours and could trust them.

People started locking their doors after Cooke.

The future Night Caller was born on 25 February 1931 in Victoria Park, Perth, to Vivian and Christine Cooke. Vivian Cooke never forgave his first-born child and only son for being born with a harelip and cleft palette. Corrective operations didn't help much. For the rest of his life Cooke had to live with his facial deformities and speech impediment. This didn't stop the elder Cooke from getting drunk every night and beating his wife, son and two daughters. When Christine tried to protect her son from the belting and head punching, Vivian would just start on her again then belt the boy even harder.

There was no peace at school either. Schoolmates constantly taunted the young Eric and the boy became a classic outcast.

In spite of good grades Cooke left school at 14 to work as a delivery boy. With most of his father's money going to pickling his liver, Cooke used his wages to help support his family.

The constant grind of poverty forced Cooke to steal food, money … anything he could lay his hands on. He was a small man who could hide in small places. Burglary came easy and he also acquired a taste for voyeurism. Sometimes, if he couldn't find anything of value in a house, he'd start a fire for kicks.

Eventually he was caught in the middle of a burglary and, starting in May 1949, served only three months of a three-year prison sentence—a concession to Cooke's crimes being motivated by poverty. After jail he worked in a factory and joined a Methodist congregation. He was arrested again when his prints were traced to a robbery at the church, but once again he was given another chance.

In July 1953, 22-year-old truck driver Cooke married 17-year-old Sarah Lavin. Together they would have four boys and three girls.

In spite of everything, 'Cookie' seemed to have grown into a likable, working-class family man, but on Friday and Saturday nights the burglaries continued. Sarah never questioned his forays. She assumed that he just wanted to be out of the house, a habit he developed as a child in order to avoid his father.

The luck didn't last. After crashing a stolen car in 1955 Cooke received two years' hard labour and wasn't released until December 1956. He soon returned to burglary, hiding his mouth with a cloth to conceal his disfigurement, in case someone saw him.

29 JANUARY 1959

While casing an apartment block in South Perth, on , Cooke saw Pnena Berkman 33, getting ready for bed. He broke into her apartment and woke Berkman up. During the ensuing fight, she scratched Cooke's face, but Cooke stabbed her with an eight-inch (20cm) diver's knife. Cooke had become a murderer.

19 DECEMBER 1959

Cooke bashed socialite Jillian Brewer, 22, with a hatchet in her Cottesloe apartment and stabbed her to death with a pair of scissors.

25 JANUARY 1960

Cooke was arrested on for loitering and sentenced to a month's hard labour in Fremantle prison.

Cooke had also become a snowdropper: a sex pervert who steals women's underwear from clotheslines, masturbates and ejaculates into them. The police suspected this, but didn't charge him through lack of evidence.

By 1963 the people of Perth were reporting more car theft, more house robberies, more peeping Tom incidents and more snowdropping. There were more women being injured in hit and runs and more assaults on women in their own beds. Eric Edgar Cooke was a respectable man by day, a one-man crime wave by night.

27 JANUARY 1963

At 2 am, poultry shop owner, Nicholas August, and barmaid, Roweena Reeves, were having a beer in a parked car near the Ocean Beach Hotel, which had just closed.

Cooke crept up on the car, but the couple notice him, decide that he's a 'perve' and tell him to 'piss off'. Cooke doesn't react so August throws an empty beer bottle at him. Cooke replied by shooting them with a .22 calibre rifle he had just stolen. The bullet passed through August's neck and hit Reeve's wrist. August managed to start the car and escape as Cooke fired another shot, which missed.

Not long afterwards Cooke found a flat in Broome Street with the door open and accountant and lifesaver, Brian Weir 29, asleep in bed, He shot him—point blank. Weir survived … barely: half paralysed and blind in one eye.

Later that morning Cooke made it to Nedlands where he found John Lindsay Sturkey 19, asleep on the veranda of a boarding house. He shot him in the head—point blank. Sturkey died instantly.

Cooke then walked to a nearby street and picked a house at random. He rang the doorbell twice. Retired grocer, George Walmsley 54, answered the door and Cooke shot him between the eyes—point blank. Walmsley fell dead. Cooke calmly dumped his stolen car and returned home at 4 am as if nothing had happened.

Police quickly established that the bullets all came from the same gun.

10 FEBRUARY 1963

Shenton Park: Cooke runs down and kills Rosemary Anderson 17, with a stolen Holden. He crashes the car into a tree in King's Park to disguise the damage of the hit and run. He wipes the blood off the car.

16 FEBRUARY 1963

West Perth: social worker, Constance Lucy Madrill, wakes to find Cooke in her room in the midst of a burglary. Cooke knocks her unconscious, strangles her to death with a light cord, removes her nightgown and has sex with her corpse. The next morning the parents of television personality, Caroline Noble, find Madrill's naked body in their backyard with an empty whisky bottle in its arms.

10 AUGUST 1963

University student, Shirley Martha McLeod 18, is studying while babysitting for a family in Dalkeith when Cooke shoots her between the eyes with the same .22 calibre rifle he's used before. When the children's parents come home at 2 am they find her body still holding a pen.

Police found one single unaccounted fingerprint at the murder scene. They fingerprinted everyone in Dalkeith. Nothing. Police said they would be prepared to fingerprint every man in Perth.

17 August 1963

An elderly couple finds a rifle hidden in a bush near the Swan River in Mount Pleasant. Police take the gun away and do a forensics check before carefully replacing it, tying the gun to the bush with fishing line. They put the bush under 24-hour surveillance. A bullet taken from the gun matches the one taken from Shirley McLeod's skull.

31 August 1963

Two weeks later, on a Saturday night, Cooke makes sure no one is looking when he retrieves the rifle. The police arrest him immediately. At first Cooke denies everything, but his wife Sarah refuses to back her husband up with an alibi.

★★★

When Cooke asked her why she said he was out on the night of McLeod's death: 'Because it's the truth, Eric, and you know it,' Sarah said.

With amazingly detailed recall of facts Cooke began an astonishing series of confessions, including 250 burglaries, dozens of car thefts, seven unsolved hit-and-runs, the assaults and the murders.

Police were shocked when they discovered that Cooke had killed Rosemary Anderson. Her boyfriend, John Button, had already been imprisoned and sentenced on 4 May 1963, to 10 years' hard labour for running her over in his 1962 Simca. Button insisted at his trial that the police had forced his confession.

Similarly, two years earlier, in August 1961, deaf-mute, convicted thief and child molester, Darryl Raymond Beamish, had already been sentenced to death (later commuted to life) for the murder of Jillian Brewer. Beamish pleaded not guilty at his trial and claimed he had no idea what he was signing under police coercion.

Strangely, Cooke retracted his confession for the murders of Anderson and Brewer two days later. On 25 November 1963, Cooke's trial began.

One of Cooke's defence team, Des Heenan, read this statement from Cooke's mother.

> 'Eric did not have a happy childhood ... He had a lot of operations and was always in and out of hospital ... His father would not really accept him. He was an unattractive child. He was a nice little boy, it was just that he wasn't normal like other children and my husband never seemed to be able to accept this. He treated him very badly. He used to beat him up for no reason at all ... He was beaten with belts, sticks and bare fists.
>
> If you publish this I am going to get into an awful lot of trouble. I have to live in the house with my husband and he is a very cruel man … The poor thing—I don't know what comes over my boy. When he was young he used to suffer from blackouts and he had a tumour of the brain. I think Mr Ainslie removed it.
>
> My husband bashed him in the head with his fist and Eric's temple hit a light switch. He had to go to hospital. I think there was a fracture or something. I think that is why Dr Ainslie had to operate on him.
>
> Since Eric has been arrested I have been forbidden to go and see him by my husband. He is wallowing in self-pity and drinking himself to death. I am sorry for my boy and I wish there was something I could do.
>
> A couple of years ago my husband attempted to murder me. He was put on a bond by the Police Court. I was taken to hospital. I had a compound fracture of the ribs and one of them was piercing my lung. I was on the danger list and a detective stayed with me. I wouldn't charge my husband because I was afraid. He works at Sydney Atkinsons in the spare parts section. I have had to work all of my married life because my husband doesn't keep me—ever since the kids were at kindy. I am not leaving him now because I have worked for the home and I don't want to

> leave him to it. On three occasions I have taken him to court for separations. On the last occasion Charles R Hopkins got a separation for me. This was about 10 years ago. I have not worried about it since, but I have been beaten up regularly. The police won't interfere.'

It made no difference in the end.

Three days later the jury took just over an hour to find him guilty of the murder of John Lindsay Sturkey. Justice Virtue sentenced Cooke to hang. As Cooke was already on Death Row, the state did not pursue trials for the other cases.

John Button and Darryl Beamish's lawyers appealed their cases. In September 1964 the High Court rejected both appeals on the grounds that Cooke had lied to prolong the investigation and delay his execution.

On 26 October 1964 at 7:50 am Eric Edgar Cooke swore on the bible to Reverend Ralph Thomas: '... before Almighty God I killed Anderson and Brewer.'

At 8:00 am as one lone protestor held a candlelight vigil outside the gates of Fremantle Prison, Cooke became the last man to be hanged in Western Australia.

He was buried in an unmarked pauper's grave at Fremantle cemetery, directly on top of child serial killer, Martha Rendall, who on 6 October 1909, had become the last woman hanged in Western Australia.

As a direct result of his injuries, Brian Weir died on 19 December 1965, almost two years after Cooke shot him.

For many years after the events, parents in Perth warned their children to lock their doors and windows 'in case Cookie comes'.

***

John Button's ordeal lasted for decades. He served 5½ years of his ten-year sentence and, once out of jail in November 1968, he began the campaign to clear his name. He got nowhere.

In 1992, however, he met author, Estelle Blackburn, who took up his cause. Six years later she published her book Broken Lives. The book generated a great controversy and John Button was finally granted the right to appeal on 17 August 1999. The Western Australian Court of Criminal Appeal (WA CCA) set down the hearing for 28 May 2001.

On 10 February 2000, the 37th anniversary of Rosemary Anderson's death and John Button's 56th birthday, the *Post Newspaper* flew University of Texas pedestrian crash expert, Rusty Haight, to Perth. *The Post* had tracked down four 1962 Simcas and a Holden of the model Cooke had used to kill Anderson. Haight conducted tests that proved that John Button was innocent: 'I could see nothing, not even the tiniest indication, that the Simca was the crash vehicle ... From the test results, taken together with all the known facts, I can say that Cooke did commit this murder.'

On 25 February 2002, on what would have been Eric Edgar Cooke's 71st birthday, the WA CCA found that Haight's tests had established reasonable doubt and overturned John Button's conviction, declaring a miscarriage of justice.

On 9 April 2003, the government of Western Australia offered John Button, then 59, a record ex-gratia payment of $460 000 in compensation for his wrongful conviction. He said that the payment would allow him and his wife to 'get on with our lives.'

He had waited over 40 years for justice.

★★★

Daryl Raymond Beamish emerged from jail in 1976, having served 15 years of a life sentence for the murder of Jillian Brewer. Again, as a result of Estelle Blackburn's book, he also won the right to appeal his conviction in June 2000.

The same lawyer, Tom Percy QC, who had worked pro bono for John Button, succeeded in clearing Daryl Beamish too. The WA CCA overturned his 1961 conviction in April 2005. Since his arrest in 1960 Beamish had waited 45 years for justice. With incredible restraint, Beamish maintains that he will not seek compensation.

It seems that Eric Edgar Cooke succeeded beyond his wildest dreams when he explained his motives: 'I just wanted to hurt somebody'.

In 2005 and 2006, Tom Percy worked tirelessly to defend convicted drug importer Schapelle Corby from a possible death sentenc. He never charged a cent.

1967: Ronald Joseph Ryan

The story of the last man to be hanged in Australia is one of politics and controversy. The case is tarnished by the fact that the state probably executed an innocent man. The case remains controversial to this day.

Born in Carlton on 21 February 1925 to Irish Catholic coalminer, John Ronald 'Big Jack' Ryan, and domestic servant, Eveline Cecilia Ryan (nee Young), Ronald Joseph Ryan's childhood was one of poverty and deprivation. Silicosis was ravaging John's lungs and he spent most of his pension on alcohol. John Ryan died in 1943.

When Ronald was 10, Child Welfare took him to an orphanage and his three younger sisters to a convent. Ron ran away at 14 and, through hard work, managed to save some money. When he was 18, Ron returned home and helped his mother and sisters as the family's sole breadwinner. In 1947 Ron married Dorothy Janet George. They had three daughters who lived to adulthood and one stillborn son. He worked hard as a timber-cutter, but by 1956, the timber season over and with no job and no money he started forging checks to pay the bills. He was caught twice and the second time was released on a good behaviour bond. He worked a series of straight jobs but supplemented his income with gambling. After Melbourne Cup Day 1959, having lost all his money, he started stealing.

Caught and sent to Bendigo prison in 1960 he made up for the education he didn't have and earned his school leaving certificate in 1962. Governor Ian Grindlay was so impressed at Ryan's efforts at self-improvement that he recommended early release. Out of jail, Ryan tried going straight again but started doing jobs as a safe-blower and, in July 1964, was sentenced to 14 years at Pentridge, where Ian Grindlay was now the governor.

Dorothy gave up on Ryan, divorced him and remarried. Ryan thought that everything would be all right if only he could leave jail with a lot of money.

He discovered that, at that time, Australia had no extradition treaty with Brazil so he hatched a plot to escape prison, rob a few banks then go to Brazil, where he could reunite the family and be safe from recapture. He planned the escape for months and behaved like a model prisoner, earning freedoms and access to what he'll need to escape. He recruited 24-year-old Peter John Walker to help him.

Ryan had served 17 months of his sentence when, at 2:00 pm on Sunday 19 December 1965—while the guards were having their Christmas lunch—he and Walker—using benches and a rope of bedspreads—made it to the prison tower where prison guard Helmut Lange was on duty. Ryan took one of the M1 carbine rifles issued to the guards and forced Lange at gunpoint to open the door to the street. Ryan and Walker made it to Sydney Road and, just as prison officer George Hodson was about to capture Walker, a single shot rang out and Hodson fell down—dead.

Ryan and Walker highjacked a blue Vanguard and made a getaway. While the media began a frenzy of stories, Ryan and Walker robbbed the ANZ in Ormond of £4500. They hid out at the house of a friend, Christine Aitken, until a friend of Christine's, truck driver James 'Boofhead' Henderson, recognised them. Walker shot Henderson and dumped his body in a public toilet in Albert Park. Christine went to the police on Christmas Eve, 1965.

Ryan and Walker bought a car with the money from the robbery and make it as far as Coogee in Sydney. Walker decided to arrange a double date for him and Ryan with an old girlfriend, nurse Simone Hurley. Walker called her … and she called the police. The men were shocked when they arrived for the date and found themselves surrounded by a police ambush. It was 5 January 1966. After seventeen days on the run it was all over. Authorities recovered the gun, the M1 carbine rifle, from the boot of the car.

Ryan was formally charged with the murder of prison guard George Hodson. He and Walker were sent back to Melbourne.

The trial opened on 15 March 1966. The judge, Justice John Starke, was a known opponent of the death penalty.

The prosecution's case was full of holes, but that didn't seem to matter.

According to the prison Duty Roster Book, Helmut Lange wasn't on duty that day, yet at the trial Lange testified that he was, in fact, working that day. Lange also testified that, while they were all in the guard tower,

Ryan seemed to be unfamiliar with the M1. Lange further stated that Ryan must have activated the bolt on the carbine while the safety catch was on. Although Lange said that he did not actually witness Ryan misusing the gun this way the guard nevertheless speculated that by doing so, Ryan would have ejected one of the bullets, leaving seven in the gun. No-one ever found that particular bullet and there were still seven bullets left in the gun when the gun was recovered.

Forensics never properly examined the gun that Ryan supposedly used to kill Hodson. No-one ever definitively established whether or not someone had even fired the alleged murder weapon in the first place.

All thirteen witnesses at the trial testified that they only heard one shot. Before the execution, four prisoners claimed that it was a prison guard shooting from a tower.

Dr Philip Opas QC defended Ryan. 'Ryan always vehemently denied to me that he shot Hodson', he said.

Convinced of Ryan's innocence he did some research. He called an expert mathematician who used a model skeleton to demonstrate that the shot that killed Hodson could not have come from ground level.

Meanwhile the media inflamed public sentiment against Ryan and Walker.

While they were deliberating the jury genuinely believed that the death penalty in Victoria was history. There had, after all, been no execution in the 16 years since the hanging of Jean Lee, Robert Clayton and Norman Andrews in February 1951. Thirty five previous death sentences had all been commuted to life imprisonment. Victoria was effectively abolitionist. Under that general misapprehension, only two jurors had originally wanted to find Ryan guilty. In the end the others agree on the verdict and, on March 30 1966, the jurors found Peter John Walker guilty of the manslaughters of George Hodson and Boofhead Henderson. Walker was sentenced to twelve years for each offence.

The jurors found Ronald Joseph Ryan guilty of the murder of Hodson. Justice John Starke had no choice but to impose a mandatory death sentence on Ryan, an act that haunted him for the rest of his life.

Opas immediately began to appeal. The first appeal was rejected. In

October 1966 another appeal was rejected. Ryan's legal aid was cut off, yet Opas continued to represent Ryan, not only without pay, but while under the shadow of death threats.

Opas flew to England to appeal to the Privy Council, which also refused appeal. On 26 January Ryan made a personal appeal to the Queen of England. This didn't work either.

State Parliament was barricaded as thousands of anti-execution demonstrators protested. Justice Starke refused a further plea for appeal. Seven jurors publicly announced that they would not have found Ryan guilty of murder if they had known he would hang. Four jurors attempted to appeal directly to the Victorian State Premier, Sir Henry Bolte, who had the power to commute the sentence. He consistently and stubbornly refused to give into public pressure to save Ryan and reopen the case. There was a state election coming up and he needed the pro-death penalty votes. Bolte cynically remarked that 'A hanging is 10 per cent of the vote'. Some 14 270 people signed a petition against the hanging. Bolte ignored it.

Cecilia, Ryan's mother wrote to Bolte: 'I plead again for the life of my son and I ask that even at this late hour you will reverse your decision to hang my son. If you cannot find it in your heart to grant this request, then I pray in your heart that you grant me one last favour, that the body of my son be given into my custody immediately after his death.'

Bolte's office simply replied, 'Your son's life will not be spared and his body will not be returned to you.'

Dorothy visited her ex-husband in Pentridge, without their daughters, to say goodbye. A few days before Ryan's execution Dorothy's second husband died of a heart attack.

Ryan learned that criminals on the outside were planning an armed breakout for him. To prevent further possible deaths, he warned the authorities.

Ryan later said 'We've all got to go sometime, but I don't want to go this way for something I didn't do.'

Ryan then wrote one last letter to his family, on toilet paper:

> 'It has been of the utmost concern to me that I have lost contact with you through what—to use a dramatic phrase—has been my darkest hour. It is my considered opinion that during crisis a family should be closer together in spirit and loyalty, presenting a closed and united front to hostile elements and affording each other—as only a family can—comfort and support. This, despite the nature and rights and wrongs of the situation.'

The day before Ryan died, his daughter, only a little girl at the time, called Opas and begged him to save Ryan's life. He couldn't.

It was eighteen days before what would have been Ryan's 42nd birthday. At 8:00 am on Friday 3 February 1967, as thousands protested outside Pentridge Prison, Governor Ian Grindlay, Prison Chaplain Father John 'Brow' Brosnan and fourteen journalists watched Ronald Joseph Ryan hang from the same gallows that killed Jean Lee sixteen years before and killed Ned Kelly eighty-six years before.

Ryan's last words were to the hangman, 'Mr Jones: God bless you, please make it quick'. It was. It took 25 seconds.

In an interview with the *Queensland Sunday Mail*, on 13 May 2001, Brian Morely, who covered the execution for radio 3AW said:

> 'It was the most callous thing I'd ever seen in my entire life and the most pathetic. It was horrendous, just horrendous ... they killed him while we watched. All the jury assumed that Ryan would get a life sentence ... It was at that point I realised they were actually going to kill a man and I was required to watch it and the absolute brutality of this event took me over ... It was so callous. It was so deliberate ... As they pulled the trapdoor lever, I had to close my eyes, I couldn't watch any more ... The hangman pulled the hood over Ryan's face and then literally leapt back and grabbed the lever ... Then there was an almighty crash that was followed by the sound of a creaking rope ... I opened my eyes to see that he was gone and the rope was swaying from the beam ... It was terribly quiet afterwards, like no one could believe it. One of the people actually went to the toilet and was physically sick

> ... I was the first to sign the witness book ... I couldn't wait to get out of the place ... It never leaves you, but the more I talk about it the better I seem to get, even after more than 30 years'.

Ryan's body was covered in quicklime and buried in an unmarked grave on the grounds of Pentridge Prison. The exact location has never been released.

As he died, prisoners in Pentridge stopped whatever they were doing and refused to work. The thousands of protestors outside the jail stood in silence for three minutes. Traffic stopped. People lit candles.

When asked what he was doing as Ryan was being hanged, Premier Bolte replied: 'Oh, I was probably having a shave, a shit or a shower'. Philip Opas resigned from the bar in protest over the whole affair.

A curse seemed to hang over the case for a while. Not long after Ryan's execution three of the guards who had given testimony favouring the prosecution died. One of them was Helmut Lange.

On 12 April 1969, while on duty at Pentridge, Lange shot himself in the head. Shortly afterwards a man with a thick German accent, claiming to have been a friend of Lange, telephoned Philip Opas and said that Lange was forced to submit a false report that no bullet had been recovered. Lange complied to keep his job. When Opas urged the man to go to the police with this information the man hung up. Opas never heard from him again.

In an interview in with the Australian Coalition Against the Death Penalty (ACADP) in 2004, Opas, then 87, said:

> 'This only confirmed for me what I have always believed, namely that Lange lied in the witness box. The ejection of the round made it impossible for Ryan to have committed the murder ... Ryan did not deserve to die ... Ryan never had a chance right from the start, the media mounted a massive campaign of fear among the public, claiming that the two escapees were extremely dangerous when actually both men were nothing more than small-time crooks'.

It has since been argued that Ryan was tried by the media and, in the climate of the time, could not get a fair trial. Ironically, after Ryan's sentencing, the media launched a united-front about-face and condemned the proposed hanging. To this day Opas defends Ryan:

> 'I will go to my grave firmly of the opinion that Ronald Ryan did not commit murder. I refuse to believe that at any time he told anyone that he did ... I am of the opinion that not only did he not fire a shot, but that he could not have fired the shot that killed Hodson. I rely on facts that could neither lie or be mistaken. The bullet that killed Hodson was never recovered. It passed right through Hodson's body. It was never proven that the M1 carbine held by Ryan ever fired a shot while in his possession'.

Opas believes that a prison guard accidentally killed Hodson, 'but a cleverly tainted conspiracy was quickly put in order to protect prison officials. I suspect a lot of people knew the truth but remained silent to protect others'. He contends that someone may have altered the prison Duty Roster Book on that day.

In 1996, newly born-again Christian, Doug Pascoe wanted to cleanse his soul and confessed on national television that he had been on duty at the Number 3 prison guard tower during the escape, contrary to the record in the Duty Roster Book. Pascoe said he fired at Ryan and may have accidentally shot Hodson. Prison authorities called Pascoe a liar. Another prison guard, Robert Paterson, was in a similar position and could also have accidentally killed Hodson.

Bolte's vote-winning strategy worked. He had been in power since 1955 and was re-elected until 1972, the longest serving Victorian Premier ever. He died in 1990.

Justice John Starke died in 1994. Pentridge Governor, Ian Grindlay, died in 1995. Prison Chaplain John Brosnan died in March 2003, aged 83.

Ryan's widow Janet died in November 2003, aged 74. She never stopped loving him.

Peter John Walker served 16 years of his 24-year sentence and was released in 1983. He has since married and now lives in country Victoria.

Pentridge prison closed in 1997. Ned Kelly also lies there in an unmarked grave.

In an interview with the ACADP, Carol Hodson, daughter of George Hodson, said that 'the hanging of Ronald Ryan did me no favours'. She remains opposed to the death penalty.

Dr Opas for one, believes that capital punishment will never be reintroduced to Australia.

The Crimes (Death Penalty Abolition) Amendment Act 1985 formally ended capital punishment in Australia.

2004: Schapelle Corby

In 2004 and 2005 the plight of ten Australians suddenly attracted international attention as they faced the death penalty in Indonesia.

On 8 October 2004, Indonesian Customs officials apprehended then 27-year-old Schapelle Corby for importing 4.1 kilos (9lb)of cannabis. The Indonesian Supreme Court confirmed her conviction and sentenced her to prison for 20 years on 19 January 2006, after an appeals court overturned her earlier sentence reduction of 15 years.

2005: The Bali Nine

The Bali Nine were arrested on 17 April 2005 for conspiring to export 8.3kgs (17.5lb) of heroin from Bali. Their fates were more or less decided between 13–15 February 2006. Only the ringleaders now sit on Death Row:

Andrew Chan, 21 (Sydney)—sentenced to death.
Myuran Sukumaran, 24 (Sydney)—sentenced to death.

As for the others, the 'drug mules':

Michael William Czugaj, 20 (Brisbane)—life imprisonment.
Renae Lawrence, 27 (Newcastle)—life imprisonment.

Tach (Tan) Duc Thanh Nguyen, 27 (Brisbane)—life imprisonment.
Matthew James Norman, 18 (Sydney)—life imprisonment.
Scott Anthony Rush, 19 (Brisbane)—life imprisonment.
Martin Eric Stephens, 29 (Wollongong)—life imprisonment.
Si Yi Chen, 20 (Sydney)—life imprisonment.

At the time of writing the Indonesian court has given them all life sentences. In Indonesia life actually means life. They could spend the rest of their lives in Kerobokan Penitentiary in Denpasar. All are appealing their sentences—a risky business in Indonesia where the courts can decrease a sentence, but may also increase it. Look what happened to Shapelle Corby, after all. Seven of the Bali nine may still face the death penalty.
There is little hope for Myuran Sukumaran and Andrew Chan. According to a report in the *Sydney Morning Herald* on 24 January 2006:

> 'The prosecutors told a Bali court there was no reason to show any leniency to Sukumaran because he had helped to organise the heroin smuggling operation and he was the one who strapped the heroin to the bodies of the drug mules … Sukumaran, a martial arts expert, has been accused of being the gang's 'enforcer'… Chief prosecutor David Adji said Sukumaran had shown no remorse for trying to smuggle more than 8kg (17.5lb) of heroin to Australia last year.'

In another report in *The Australian*, 16 February 2006, Judge Suryowati, one of three presiding judges, said:

> 'In my heart I didn't want to give death, but that is the duty of the judge … In my career I've never wanted to give the death penalty.' Tears welled in her eyes as her colleague Chief Judge Lanang Dauh announced that Sukumaran would be executed.

According to another report in *The New Zealand Herald*, 16 February 2006, Myuran Sukumaran and Andrew Chan may die 'grim, lonely deaths.'

> If their executions are consistent with the pattern established with the last three drug runners executed in Indonesia, we can expect the authorities to remove Chan and Sukumaran from their cells 'with the minimum of warning', drive them to a deserted beach or jungle clearing and shoot them, without ceremony, by firing squad. No one will be told in advance of the date or time of their executions.

In the week preceeding 29 April 2006, Denpasar High Court judges confirmed death sentences for Andrew Chan and Myuran Sukumaran and the life sentence for Martin Stephens. They reduced the life sentences of Renae Lawrence, Michael Czugaj, Matthew Norman, Si Yi Chen and Tan Duc Thanh Nguyen to 20 years, citing that these five played only minor roles in the attempted drug smuggling. At the time of publication Bali prosecutors and Indonesian Attorney-General Abdul Rahman Singh planned to appeal.

In the Indonesian legal system the appeals could yet be overturned. There is still a risk that all the Bali Nine may face the death penalty.

***

Three other Australians are also on Death Row:

Talaal Adrey, Kuwait: charged and faces death sentence.
Nguyen Van Chinh, Vietnam: convicted and sentenced to death.
Mai Cong Thanh, Vietnam: convicted and sentenced to death.

With the exception of Adrey, who Kuwaiti authorities charged with being a member of the terrorist group, *The Peninsula Lions*, the other Australians are all on drug charges.

[Ed. The death sentences for Nguyen Van Chinh and Mai Cong Thanh were commuted to life in prison after clemency was granted on 18 February 2006.]

More Modern Mayhem

1989

Killer Charm: Ted Bundy

The serial killer phenomenon has been with us throughout history. There is one big difference, however, between the killers of old and the killers of new. With the advent of modern communications we started to hear a lot more about things and with television we are destined to see a lot more. What' more, the pictures move. As crazy as HH Holmes or Albert Fish might have been, at most they were just photographs. With television came the opportunity to see and hear real-life walking, talking psychopaths in the comfort, privacy and safety of your own living room. One of the most familiar faces would come to be Ted Bundy.

It was incredibly ironic that when 22-year-old Eleanor Louise Cowell gave birth to her son in a home for unwed mothers on 24 November 1946, she chose to name him 'Theodore Robert'. Theodore means 'gift of God'. Ted certainly thought he was God's gift to women: history has judged otherwise. Narcissistic, manipulative and superficially charming like all true psychopath/sociopaths, at the time of his death Ted Bundy was probably the most hated man in America. No mean feat.

Eleanor lied to Ted, telling him she was his sister and that his grandparents were his real Mom and Pop. In 1950 she and her 'brother' settled in Tacoma, Washington where she changed Ted's surname to Nelson only to change it again when she married military cook, Johnny Culpepper

Bundy on 19 May 1951. Ted was never close to his stepfather and remained closer to his grandfather, Sam.

Aside from some confusion about his relationship with his family Ted seemed to have a normal childhood, apart from a habit of stealing and burglary.

It's unknown exactly when Ted started killing young women (see below), but what is certain is that in 1966 he met Stephanie Brooks at the University of Washington and fell in whatever passed for love in Ted's soul with the beautiful girl who wore her straight, dark hair long and parted in the middle. Accounts generally agree that Ted ruined their relationship with game playing and manipulation to compensate for his own perceived inadequacies. When Stephanie broke up with him he was apparently devastated.

In 1969, Ted visited his birthplace, Burlington, Vermont, and discovered the truth he had long suspected, that his 'sister' was his mother. The records also showed a father, 'Lloyd Marshal'—an identity who may or may not have actually been real.

A return to Washington University and a failed attempt to win back Stephanie later, Bundy turned from a mediocre academic performer to an honours student.

Later in 1969, while volunteering on a crisis hotline, he met Ann Rule, the friend who would later write the definitve book on Bundy: *The Stranger Beside Me*. He also met Liz Kendall, a divorced mother with one daughter. Liz would be Bundy's girlfriend throughout most of the murders. She is known as 'Meg Anders' in Rule's book.

In 1973 Bundy graduated with a degree in psychology. About this time he again met up with Stephanie Brooks. Brooks, who was completely ignorant of Liz Kendall, was so enamoured with the new version of Bundy that they even discussed marriage.

Later that year the attacks and murders began in earnest. The full list of the women who Ted Bundy assaulted, injured, raped, tortured, maimed and killed will probably never be known. Bundy often hinted that there were more victims than police gave him credit for.

★★★

Here is one list, in chronological order. In some cases the details below demonstrate the typical Bundy way of doing things. Many of the victims were slim, young, attractive girls with straight, long brown hair, parted in the middle.

Please note the order of information: name of victim, age, place of disappearance, date of disappearance and presumed death, date and place of finding of body or remains. The date of the murder and the date of the discovery of the body or remains are the same, unless otherwise stated. Not all details are listed in all cases. Bundy is known to have committed murders in at least seven states, yet the authorities seemed to rely more on luck than on a system to track him down.

WASHINGTON STATE:

Lonnie Trumbull—Seattle—23 June 1966—Beaten to death, on the head in her sleep, probably with a piece of wood later found in a vacant lot. Attacker seriously injured her roommate, Lisa Wick, who remained in a coma for some time and remembered nothing when she awoke. Bundy denied involvement, but the attack was entirely consistent with his later pattern.

Joni Lenz, 18—Seattle—5 January 1974. Bundy entered and exited Lenz's flat through an unlocked basement window, beat her on the head and face with a bed frame rod and violently jabbed her with a vaginal probe. Lenz, 18, survived with brain damage and injuries to her internal organs.

Lynda Ann Healy, 21—Seattle—abducted 1 February 1974. Her bed was bloodstained, sheets and pillowcase missing. A semen stain on her bed was never tested, nor was her room dusted for fingerprints. Her body wasn't found until 3 March 1975. Before his execution, Bundy admitted to killing her.

Later that month, Bundy, without giving any reason, dumped Stephanie Brooks, who never saw or heard from him again. In autumn 1974 Bundy entered the University of Utah Law School, but soon dropped out.

Donna Gail Manson, 19—Olympia—12 March 1974. Bundy admitted that unidentified bones found in March 1975 were hers.

Bundy often behaved as if he wanted to be caught. Various witnesses described, at different times and different places, a man driving a VW who introduced himself as 'Ted'.

OREGON

Roberta Kathleen Parks, 20—Oregon—6 April 1974. Remains found 3 March 1975.

WASHINGTON STATE

Susan Elaine Rancourt, 19—Ellensburg—17 April 1974. Remains found 3 March 1975.

Brenda Baker, 15—Seattle—25 May 1974. Found 17 June 1974.

Brenda Carol Ball, 22—Burien—1 June 1974. Remains found 1 March 1975.

Georgeann Hawkins, 18—Seattle—11 June 1974.

Janice Ott, 23—Lake Sammamish State Park—14 July 1974. Found 6 September 1974.

Denise Naslund, 18—Lake Sammamish State Park—14 July 1974. Found 6 September 1974.

IDAHO

'Jane Doe'—Boise—21 September 1974.

UTAH

Nancy Wilcox, 16—Utah—2 October 1974.

Melissa Smith, 17—Midvale—18 October 1974. Body found 27 October 1974.

Laura Aimee, 17—Lehi—31 October 1974. Body found 27 November 1974.

Carol DaRonch, 19—Salt Lake City: attacked and abducted by Bundy but escaped on 8 November 1974. However Bundy succeeded in abducting ...

Debbie Kent, 17—in Bountiful later that day (8 November).

COLORADO

Caryn Campbell, 24—Aspen—12 January 1975. Body found 18 February 1975.
Julie Cunningham, 26—Vail—15 March 1975.
Denise Oliverson, 24—Grand Junction—6 April 1975.
Melanie Cooley, 18—Nederland—15 April 1975. Body found 23 April 1975.

IDAHO

Lynette Culver, 13—Pocatello—6 May 1975. Bundy told the FBI that he had snatched a girl from a playground, killed her and then dumped her body in the Snake River. He never knew her name and her body was never found.

UTAH

Susan Curtis, 15—Salt Lake City—28 June 1975.
Nancy Baird, 23—Layton—4 July 1975.

COLORADO

Shelley K Robertson, 24—Golden—1 July 1975. Body found 21 August 1975, in a mineshaft near Berthoud Pass.

At this point, on 16 August 1975 Bundy was arrested in Salt Lake City, during a traffic stop, for possession of burglary tools.

UTAH

Debbie Smith—Salt Lake City—February 1976. Body found 1 April at Salt Lake International Airport.

On 3 March 1976 Bundy was found guilty of the aggravated kidnapping of Carol DaRonch. On 30 June 1976 he was sentenced to 1–15 years in prison. Evidence connects him to the murder of Caryn Campbell. While preparing for trial in that case he escaped from the Pitkin County Law Library on 7 June 1977, but police tracked him down in Aspen Colorado on 13 June. Bundy then managed to escape again from Garfield County Jail in Greenwood Springs, Colorado and went to Chicago, where he stole a car and fled to Florida.

FLORIDA

On 15 January 1978, Ted Bundy attacked the Chi Omega Sorority House in Tallahassee.

Margaret Bowman, 21—Clubbed and strangled to death.

Lisa Levy, 20—Clubbed and strangled to death. He bit off her left nipple, but a bite mark on her left buttock made such a good impression that forensic experts later used it to identify him.

While there, he also battered **Kathy Kleiner,** 21 and **Karen Chandler**, 21.

Minutes after the Chi Omega murders he battered **Cheryl Thomas**, 21, in her apartment.

Finally, he abducted **Kimberly Ann Leach**, 12, from her junior high school in Lake City on 9 February 1978. He bones were later found in an old pigpen near Suwannee River State Park. Evidence suggested she had been strangled and repeatedly raped, before and after death.

After killing Kimberly Leach, Bundy stole an orange VW and shortly after 1:00 am on 15 February 1978 he was stopped in Pensacola for speeding. In the VW police discovered a pair of handcuffs, a length of rope, a crowbar, a ski mask, an ice pick and a nylon stocking. They arrested Bundy under suspicion of burglary.

OTHER POSSIBLE BUNDY VICTIMS INCLUDE

Anne Marie Burr—the nine-year-old disappeared from her home in Tacoma on the morning of 16 August 1961. Bundy was only 15 at the time, but he knew Burr and lived only ten blocks away. He denied any involvement in Anne Marie's disappearance but many believe she was his first victim. Anne Marie's body was never found.

Rita Curran, 24—beaten on the head, raped, strangled and found by her roommate in their apartment on 19 July 1971. Rita worked in a hotel next door to the building in which Bundy was born.

Rita Lorraine Jolly, 17—disappeared from West Linn, Oregon, June 1973.
Vicky Lynn Hollar, 24—disappeared from Eugene, Oregon, August 1973. Oregon investigators suspected Bundy in both the Jolly and Hollar cases, but never had an opportunity to interrogate him about them.
Carol Valenzuela and **'Jane Doe'**—both found near a deer path outside Vancouver, Washington, on 12 October, 1974. Estimated deaths early September 1974.

Seen as a whole, Bundy's crimes give the impression of reckless abandon, constant movement and an ever-increasing disregard for human life or even his own self-preservation. Frequently living off his wits and the proceeds of burglary, his behaviour was often erratic, yet he still managed to systematically stalk or lure young women to their deaths. One of his favourite ploys was to put his arm in a sling, ask a young woman for help carrying something and then attack her. He later said: ' ... I'm the most cold-blooded sonovabitch you'll ever meet ... Sometimes I feel like a vampire.'

Throughout his trials for the Florida murders he ran the gamut from placidity to violence. He even conducted his own defence, although that tactic failed spectacularly when it became obvious to the jury that he appeared to be relishing and reliving the murders when he asked police to describe them in court.

Yet what people say over and over again is that he was charming. Even Judge Edward Cowart said to him, while sentencing him to death: 'You're a bright young man. You'd have made a good lawyer and I'd have loved to have you practice in front of me, but you went the wrong way, partner. Take care of yourself. I don't have any animosity to you. I want you to know that. Take care of yourself.'

On 2 July 1979 he was found guilty of the murders of Margaret Bowman and Lisa Levy. On 31 July he was sentenced to death. On 6 February 1980 he was found guilty of the murder of his last victim, Kimberly Leach. Even before he was sentenced to death for her murder on 9 February he knew it was over. 'It's no use. We've lost the jury. There's no point in playing their game,' he said.

Bundy spent almost nine years on Death Row, often providing psychologists with a lot of information, writing and frequently referring to himself in the third person, as if someone else had committed all those attacks and murders.

He became famous for playing a continuous game of cat-and-mouse with both authorities and the public. He liked to give the impression that he was totally in control. He was certainly the centre of attention, and he seemed to relish it. Everything about Bundy became a dramatic, bizarre circus. Highlights of his years on Death Row included the following:

- While on trial for the Leach murder he exploited an old Florida law that declares a couple married—if they take their vows under oath. He called Carole Ann Boone 'a former co-worker and admirer' to the witness stand. He asked her to marry him. She said yes. The marriage was legal. Somehow, during a jail visit they conceived a daughter, who was born in October 1982. Boone later divorced Bundy, however, and changed her and her daughter's last name.
- In 1981, Bundy's long-time girlfriend, Liz Kendall, published The Phantom Prince, My Life with Ted Bundy.
- In 1984, King County officials admitted that they had lost the remains of Denise Naslund and Janice Ott. In 1987, they paid the victims' families $224 000 in compensation.
- Bundy's execution was stayed on 2 July 1986, only fifteen minutes before he was scheduled to die, and again on 18 November 1986, seven hours before his scheduled execution.
- In late 1988 Bundy began a spate of confessions to buy himself another stay of execution. The ploy failed.
- The night before he died Bundy gave an interview to Dr James Dobson, head of the Christian group Focus on the Family. Bundy blamed pornography, how it helped to 'shape and mould' him to commit 'behaviour too terrible to describe'. He also blamed booze, 'What alcohol did in conjunction with exposure to pornography is: alcohol

> reduced my inhibitions at the same time the fantasy life that was fuelled by pornography eroded them further'. He also said that, while actually committing the murders, he was possessed by 'something ... awful and alien. There is just absolutely no way to describe, first the brutal urge to do that kind of thing, and then what happens is—once it has been more or less satisfied and recedes—you might say, or spent, that energy level recedes and basically I become myself again.'

His time finally ran out when he was executed in the electric chair at 7:16 am on 24 January 1989, at Florida State Prison.

His last meal was one steak, two eggs, a serving of hash browns and a cup of coffee.

His last words were: 'I'd like you to give my love to my family and friends.'

By the time they were finished with him, American taxpayers had spent well over US$8 million dollars on Bundy.

As a final irony his executioner was rumoured to be a woman.

***

For many years Bill and Sally Devine thought that Ted Bundy had killed their 14-year-old-daughter, Katherine Merry Devine. She disappeared from Seattle on 25 November 1973. On 6 December 1973 her body was found, lying face down, throat slashed, her pants cut open from the waist to the crotch. In 2003 William E Cosden Jr was convicted of her murder, based largely on 28-year-old DNA evidence.

Ted Bundy had always denied killing Kathy Devine.

1994

A Mistake of Nature: Andrei Chikatilo

A socialist idyll or communist utopia isn't supposed to be a place where you find serial killers. After all, such things are the product of 'decadent Western imperialism' and could never happen in the USSR. Was it this general attitude—as well as the spirit of the place and time—that fostered the reign of the Red Ripper?

Andrei Romanovich Chikatilo was born in a small village in the Ukraine in 1936, not long after a major famine in the region. His mother regularly reminded Andrei that his elder brother, Stepan, had been abducted when he was 10 and eaten by starving peasants. This disturbing story was never corroborated.

Chikatilo seemed to grow up normally enough. He married and had two children. By all accounts he was a good husband and a good father. He was a university-educated schoolteacher and later, a factory materials buyer.

In September 1982, the mutilated and mostly decomposed body of 13-year-old Lyubov Biryuk was found near Novorcherkassk in the Ukraine. The autopsy showed that she had been attacked from behind, hit on the back of the head and stabbed 22 times. Two ribs were broken and a knife had gouged her eyes out of their sockets. Over the next eight years, locals found the remains of many other victims in or around

Rostov-on-Don. Typically the remains were lying facedown and all showed the same vicious stabbing and eye-gouging patterns.

Major Mikhail Fetisov and Lieutenant Viktor Burakov were involved with the case from the beginning, but they were frequently at odds with their nominal superiors and regional colleagues who demonstrated varying degrees of incompetence and negligence. The investigation was long, protracted and eccentric. Chikatilo was eclectic in his choice of victims. He targeted women as old as their 50s, young men, girls and boys as young as eight. At one point the authorities believed that they were dealing with a number of copycat murderers.

The number of male victims gave the authorities an excuse to persecute some homosexuals. One man hanged himself when he learned he was a suspect. One man, a known sex offender, was executed for a murder Chikatilo had actually committed. Another man, Yuri Kalenik, 19, spent five years in custody, under suspicion. Over the years a number of people—including mentally retarded men—confessed to the killings, sometimes under duress, but the forensic reports and their stories consistently didn't add up.

By mid 1984, 24 victims had emerged, all killed in a similar manner.

For years evidence accumulated that something was seriously wrong in Rostov, yet the authorities, the *militsia*, refused to officially acknowledge that the ever-increasing number of maimed, mutilated and cannibalised bodies was the work of a serial killer.

In communist Ukraine the press were prevented from talking about the links between the murders. The media weren't even allowed to give the public details to warn them of the danger they were in.

While the number of bodies began to reach embarrassing levels a Major Zanasovsky, working undercover, was casing Rostov bus station when he observed Chikatilo accost several women. Eventually Chikatilo engaged a prostitute to give him oral sex under his coat. Zanasovsky arrested him on the spot for indecent behaviour. Police inspected his briefcase and found a long kitchen knife, a piece of rope, a jar of Vaseline and a dirty towel.

Although he was detained for two days, Chikatilo denied any involvement in the area killings. Since the police had nothing further on him they had to release him. Chikatilo was free again to kill for over five more years.

Frustrated, Burakov consulted Moscow psychiatrist, Alexandr Bukhanovsky, on several occasions. Bukhanovsky eventually profiled the killer as one male, a loner between 45 and 50 and around 5ft 10ins (1.8cm) tall, a heterosexual yet compulsive sexual deviate and necrosadist who brutalised his victims for arousal, killed them for gratification and blinded them to stop them seeing how inadequate he was. He was an arrogant, narcissistic planner, definitely not retarded or schizophrenic. The stabbings were a symbolic way to enter his victims sexually.

Killing his victims gave Chikatilo the arousal he couldn't find anywhere else. His favourite practices included:

- Repeated stabbings—in one case a young man had been stabbed 70 times
- Cutting out tongues
- Disembowelment with knivesa
- Disembowelment with bare hands
- Biting off nipples
- Cutting off boys' genitals, throwing them into the woods or eating the testicles
- Ejaculating into women's genitals, cutting them off and eating these 'truffles of a sexual murder'

For 10 months the killings stopped, then in August 1985 a body near Moscow led to more false leads.

Burakov went so far as to consult Anatoly Slivko, who was convicted of the sexual murder of seven boys. Slivko provided Burakov with an insight into the mind of a serial killer—a mind so compartmentalised that it lived a double life—even the people closest to him would suspect nothing. Hours after his conversation with Burakov, Slivko was executed.

Other bodies turned up and an exhausted Burakov had a nervous breakdown at the end of 1986. Strangely, nothing happened for almost 18 months until 6 April 1988 when a railroad worker found the nude body of a woman. More time passed and more victims were found: still no more leads.

The proletariat paradise—which had created the Red Ripper and hampered the investigation with needless secrecy and red tape, allowing Chikatilo to thrive—virtually collapsed, along with the Berlin wall, in 1989. The abolition of the Communist Party in February 1990 and a new Russia meant that Chikatilo started running out of time.

Chikatilo liked to target 'lower class undesirables'. These telling terms give an insight into the more prissy aspects of Chikatilo's compartmentalised personality. Author Peter Vronsky didn't know it at the time, but while in Moscow to film a documentary in 1990 he met Chikatilo. In his book, *Serial Killers*, Vronsky described that the man—who had already killed and tortured dozens—was in the capital to protest the illegal building of a garage and toilet beneath his son's apartment. He said it was a conspiracy. A few days later Chikatilo lured a mentally-handicapped 16-year-old boy off a train in Rostov and took him to a wood where he tied the boy up, ripped of his clothes, raped him, bit off the tip of his tongue, stabbed him many times in the head and stomach, cut off his genitals and threw them in the trees.

Ten days after that he did virtually the same thing with another 16-year-old boy. A week after that he killed his last known victim, a 22-year-old woman. A policeman saw him at the tap at the railroad station washing off what he thought was blood. The policeman questioned him, recorded his ID and let him go. The police put him under surveillance, however, and picked him up shortly after the body of the woman was found a few days later.

At first Chikatilo would admit nothing. Then Alexandr Bukhanovsky, who had provided Burakov with such an insightful profile, read the profile to Chikatilo. Confronted by a man who seemed to look into his most secret self, Chikatilo confessed. It had begun with the murder of nine-year-old Yelena Zakotnova, in early 1978. Chikatilo remembered and gave accurate details of all the crimes for which he was accused. He led police to even more bodies and often re-enacted the killings for them at the various sites. Later those interviewing him would comment on his pungent, goaty odour—perhaps the result of his cannibalism. He said that seeing the blood gave him the greatest satisfaction. He eventually confessed to 56 murders but only 53 were corroborated: 31 females and 22 males. At his trial he claimed 70 victims over the twelve years he was active.

His trial began on 14 April 1992 and 225 volumes of evidence were stacked up against him. The courtroom was filled with the families of his victims. Chikatilo completely gave in to the role of the homicidal, cannibalistic and totally out-of-control lunatic. Caged in and out of court he beat himself against the bars, rattled them, screamed curses and insults, spat and raved in the way everyone expects murderous maniacs to behave—an effect heightened by his now shaved head. On two occasions he exposed himself.

His wife, Fayima, had never seen this side of him.

Chikatilo was quoted as saying: 'I am a mistake of nature, a mad beast'.

The Russian legal system differs in many ways from Western or Anglo Common Law. Throughout the trial the judge, Leonid Akubzhanov, took a very active role in questioning witnesses. Chikatilo never stood a chance. Akubzhanov even dismissed bizarre forensic results which showed that semen samples found on the bodies conflicted in tissue type with Chikatilo's blood type.

At the end of the trial, Chikatilo refused to speak.

The judge took two months to reach a verdict, but on 14 October found Chikatilo guilty of five counts of molestation and fifty-two counts of confirmed murder. He was sentenced to be shot. The relatives of his victims wanted to tear him apart with their bare hands.

On 15 February 1994 a guard led him into a special, bare concrete, soundproof room with a drain in the centre of the floor. The guard shot him behind the right ear. Citizen X, the Maniac, the Red Ripper was dead.

In the area of Rostov, population 1.5 million, in the decade 1989–99 twenty-nine multiple murderers and rapists were caught, giving Rostov the label 'serial-killer capital of the world'.

Dr Alexandr Bukhanovsky continued to work with serial killers. The 30 January 1999 edition of the *Moscow Times* published a story in which Bukhanovsky claimed he could cure violent psychopaths and has gone so far as to work with active killers who are still at large. He said his study would help reveal the roots of aggression. He would give no further details because he could not break the confidence of the killers in his care.

1994

The Clown Who Killed: John Wayne Gacy Jr

The ongoing debate about whether or not killers are born or made will never be resolved because the debate asks the wrong question. Killers are both born and made. The more interesting question is: how? How do you make a killer? One way is to make someone feel so inadequate that no matter what they do it's never good enough. Abuse though, will only turn you into a loser. It doesn't necessarily turn you into a serial killer. To become a serial killer, you need to make the decision that you feel the most alive when you are taking somebody else's life. Maybe that's why so much killing is sexual. A force to create life feeds a force for its destruction.

Working-class alcoholic and wife beater, John Wayne Stanley Gacy, and Marion Gacy gave birth to their only son—the second of their three children—klutzy, epileptic John Wayne Gacy Jr on March 17 1942 in Chicago. Gacy's inadequacies as a child didn't stand a chance against his father's frequent emotional and physical abuse.

Who knows what more might have happened if the older man had known that his son was a closet homosexual whose first sexual experience, with a teenage girl ended abruptly when he fainted?

Gacy compensated for being less-than-perfect in his father's eyes by being a workaholic, solid citizen. So much so that by 1968 he was husband to Marilynn Myers, father of two and ran three Kentucky Fried Chicken outlets for his father-in-law in Waterloo, Iowa.

The first signs of trouble started when he was convicted that year of sodomising 15-year-old Mark Miller, who worked at one of his restaurants. His wife divorced him the day he was sentenced. In 1970, he was released on account of good behaviour, having served only 18 months of a ten-year sentence. John Gacy Sr died while his son was in prison.

Gacy Jr started working in a restaurant and moved into a 1950's brick house at 8213 West Summerdale Avenue in the Chicago suburb of Norwood Park, half owned by him, half owned by his mother and his two sisters.

Gacy soon began cruising around the city, enticing, hiring or abducting young men and boys, taking them home and having sex with them.

One night in early 1972, a drunk Gacy picked up a drifter from Omaha Nebraska, Tim McCoy. Gacy claimed that, after they had sex, he fell asleep. When he woke up, McCoy was coming at him with a knife. In self-defence Gacy killed McCoy. As McCoy died, Gacy had an orgasm. Fearing that the police would never believe his self-defence claim after his previous conviction, Gacy buried McCoy in the crawlspace beneath his house.

Gacy married his second wife, Carole Hoff, a divorced mother of two daughters on 1 June 1972. He was slightly more honest with her than he'd been with his first wife. He explained his prison past to Carole and she was generous enough to believe that his troubles were all in his past. However, what he failed to explain—both to her, her children or to the neighbours they often invited to dinner parties—was the source of the strong smell coming from under the house. Gacy blamed moisture build-up.

In 1974 Gacy formed a small contract construction company, PDM, and became financially successful. He told friends he liked to hire young men because they were cheap. In reality he used the business as a way of luring 'beddable' young men—with the promise of work—into his home for 'interviews'.

In 1975 Gacy became involved in local politics and started dressing up as 'Pogo the Clown' to entertain children in hospitals and at charity events. By 1976 his marriage to Carole fell apart when Gacy started openly reading gay pornography around the house. He had killed six young men that year.

After Carole left, neighbours would occasionally hear screams from the vicinity of Gacy's house, but since all the houses in the area were on large lots, it was difficult to pick the source of the noise. On at least two occasions victims escaped Gacy. On 22 May 1978 he abducted Jeffrey Ringall, luring him with marijuana before assaulting him with chloroform. Ringall remembered being in a room where a fat man showed him some dildoes and described how he was going to use them on him. The man drugged, tortured and raped him. The next morning he woke up fully clothed under a statue in Lincoln Park, amazed that he had survived. In the absence of any further information, the police could do nothing.

Gacy came to the serious attention of police when the mother of 15-year-old Robert Peist reported her son missing on 11 December 1978. She was waiting to pick up her son from his work at a local pharmacy when he told her that a man named Gacy had offered him a job and he would be back in a minute. She never saw her son again. Police were able to obtain a search warrant and on 13 December 1978, during Gacy's absence, found in his house, among other things: gay porn, handcuffs, an 18-inch (45cm) rubber dildo, a receipt for a roll of film and some marijuana. Police were highly suspicious, but were unable to connect any of the items to Robert Peist. They arrested Gacy for possession of marijuana and only then found out about his previous conviction. They discovered that several boys who had worked for Gacy had also disappeared. Investigators established that the receipt for the film roll belonged to a co-worker of Robert Peist. Knowing the game was over, on 22 December, Gacy finally confessed to killing at least 30 people and burying the bodies under the crawlspace of his house. Police found bodies, some in such advanced stages of putrefaction they were a health hazard to dig up. Gacy had buried 27 bodies under the crawlspace. Others were buried under his garage and barbecue pit. Four more were dumped in the nearby Des Plains River. Police found bodies with underwear lodged in their throats and nooses around their necks. In their efforts to be thorough, authorities virtually demolished the house.

Gacy played games with authorities from the beginning, claiming among other stories that his alter ego called 'Jack Hanley' actually committed the rapes, tortures and murders. His lawyers tried an insanity plea, but on 12 March 1980, after only two hours deliberation, jurors found him guilty of all 33 counts of murder. Gacy was sentenced to 21 life terms and 12 death sentences.

Some of Gacy's victims were never identified. These are the names and ages of some of the ones who were. The author apologises for any inaccuracies or omissions.

Tommy Baling: 20 years old
Michael Bonnin: 17
Matthew Bowman: 19
John Butkovich: 18
William Carroll: 16
Robert Gilroy: 18
Gregory Godzik: 17
Richard Johnston: 17
William Kindred
Frank Wayne 'Dale' Landingin: 19
James 'Mojo' Mazzara: 20
Tim McCoy
John Mowery: 19
Russell Nelson: 20
Timothy O'Rourke
Robert Piest: 15
Jon Prestige: 20
Randall Reffett: 15
Darrell Sampson: 16
Samuel Stapleton: 14
John Szyc: 19
David Talsma: 19
Robert Winch: 16

The unidentified were buried in a mass ceremony on 8 June 1981, with markers inscribed 'We Are Remembered.'

By April 1979, the last of Gacy's house had been cleared away. For years nothing, not even weeds, would grow on the empty lot. Later, new owners built another house on the site, with a new address. The grass grew again.

Gacy spent 14 years on Death Row at the Menard Correctional Institution, launching one stalling appeal after another. His case cost taxpayers well over US$1 million. While in jail he wrote letters—thousands of them—and he produced oil paintings.

He also wrote two books—*They Call Him Mr Gacy: Selected Correspondence of John Wayne Gacy* and the extremely rare *A Question of Doubt* in which Gacy gave his own, self-serving, version of events.

On Monday 10 May 1994 at 12:40 am at the Stateville Penitentiary near Joliet, Illinois, John Wayne Gacy, 52, was executed by lethal injection. Many family members of his victims attended his execution as witnesses. Killing him took 18 minutes because one of the chemicals became clogged in a tube.

His last meal was shrimp, hot chips, fried chicken, a Diet coke and strawberries although he reportedly originally asked for a lobster and an iguana. His last words were 'Kiss my ass'.

2001

Method in Madness: Javed Iqbal

We seldom hear about murder in the third world or, to be more politically correct, in the 'emerging economies'. The combination of a lack of media infrastructure, the lack of a free press, the barrier of language and, above all, a reluctance on the part of certain nations to appear barbaric on the world stage, all conspire to make it very difficult to know what's going on. Then there's the general law of disaster journalism. One local death equals five deaths in your state equals 10 deaths in your country equals 20 deaths in the 'mature economies' equals 100 deaths anywhere else. Pakistan had to work really hard to grab our attention.

Javed Iqbal was a serial killer with the soul of a bureaucrat and the methodology of an accountant. He came, after all, from a wealthy and respected family who probably knew how to keep tallies and sound records.

Iqbal had a history. He'd been caught at least three times sexually abusing young boys. He bribed his way out or was released 'on bail'. Occasionally his sex life attracted attention, but when Iqbal's neighbours complained, he'd simply move away.

He started killing in mid-1999. To help him, he enlisted three teenagers: Zafar Ahmed, Mohammad Shabir, Shahzad Sajid and one young man, Ishaq Billa.

Iqbal's method didn't vary much. He would trawl the streets, often around the market square that surrounds the Mina-e-Pakistan minaret in central Lahore. In a city of seven million, he was as invisible as the boys he was looking for.

After finding a suitably vulnerable boy—typically a homeless street urchin—he would take him back to his badly-lit, poorly-ventilated, three-room house with iron gratings on the windows. There he would offer the boy a drink spiked with a sedative. As the boys relaxed he asked them questions: 'Who are you? Who is your family? Where do you live? What do you do?' He took meticulous notes. Whether he did this to gain their trust or as part of a sadistic ritual, we don't know.

We know that when the boys were sedate enough he would rape them. Then, using an iron chain, he would slowly strangle them. Sometimes he made them inhale a mixture of cyanide and acid. He would then cut up the bodies and place them in a vat filled with a mixture of hydrochloric and sulphuric acid. He would patiently wait until the bones and hair were all dissolved. He first started dumping the liquefied remains in the sewer, then—when the neighbours complained about the stench—he started to use the Ravi River near his house.

Iqbal would keep his victims' shoes and clothing in plastic bags. After his 43rd victim, he started taking photographs of the boys, often moments before he killed them. Iqbal even noted that it cost him 120 rupees (US$2.40) to 'erase' each victim.

The neighbours never seemed to notice. In a culture where men often keep boys as a combination of domestic servant and sex slave, he might have evaded detection forever, but when he reached his target of 100 boys, Iqbal wrote to *The Daily Jang*, Pakistan's largest circulating Urdu language newspaper. On 22 November 1999 the *Jang's* crime reporter received Iqbal's long and detailed confession, telling the paper where to go and what they would find there:

> 'I sexually assaulted 100 children before killing them ... All the details of the murders are contained in the diary and the 32-page notebook that have been placed in the room and has also been sent to the authorities. This is my confessional statement'.

Although the police received a copy of the confession before *The Daily Jang* received theirs, the police threw their copy away. It was only after the police knew the media were on their way that they bothered to go to Iqbal's house. The media though, were already there. They'd already found bloody handprints on the walls and floor, a gallery of photographs, 85 pairs of shoes, clothing, and the liquefied remains of two boys—the only remains of Iqbal's victims that anyone ever found—in an acid drum left open outside the house. Near the drum a card in Iqbal's own hand: 'The bodies in the house have deliberately not been disposed of so that authorities will find them.'

Iqbal, however, had disappeared. His confession said that he planned to commit suicide by drowning in the Ravi. This turned out to be a lie.

The police launched the biggest manhunt in Pakistani history up to that time. Iqbal's accomplices tried to cash a traveller's cheque in Sohowa and were arrested. Ishaq Billa, who had provided a lot of the acid, 'committed suicide' by throwing himself out of a third floor window. Journalist Irfan Husain of the English language newspaper Dawn, observed: 'even after the case had been handed to the police on a platter, the best they could do was carelessly lose an alleged accomplice of the killer ... one would imagine that by now the police would have thought of a better cover-up for death in custody'.

Parents were outraged at the police's incompetence and continuing failure to find the man. One said: 'Because we are poor, nothing is being done.'

As the manhunt went on and knowing of Billa's fate, Iqbal feared for his life if he went directly to the police. On 30 December 1999 he surrendered at the offices of *Jang*. Imagine John Wayne Gacy surrendering to the *Chicago Tribune* and you get the general idea.

Under questioning Iqbal gave several contradictory and confused versions of his story: that the confession he wrote to *The Daily Jang* and the documentation they found in his house was a fiction designed to condemn a society that treated children worthlessly; that he had taken boys into his home as servants only to be exploited by them; that after his arrest in 1998 he had embarked on a program of murder to avenge his mother who had died of the shame of his false accusations of sodomy. He said: 'Then I prayed that if I left the world, I would leave it with dozens of others ... My prayer was accepted by God and friends became angels for me and then a blood-curdling drama began. Now 100 mothers will die mourning the deaths of their children.'

Whatever else happened, Iqbal made one point clear. Of the 100 children he killed only 25 were reported missing. In Pakistan, 50 million people live below the poverty line. One less child is one less mouth to feed. Some estimate as many as 10 000 children run away from home *each year.* Many of those who live end up as bonded labourers and some 4000 land in jail. Even when they did care the parents knew the police would do nothing, they might even end up interrogated or arrested themselves. In a *Time Magazine* interview on 27 December 1999, one mother said: 'It never even occurred to me to go to the police for help.'

The two-month trial was a media circus—the courtroom packed with relatives and guards. Some family members fainted as the details of Iqbal's crimes came out. Iqbal pleaded not guilty—105 witnesses testified that he was.

On 16 March 2000, Judge Allah Baksh Ranja pronounced sentence: 'Javed Iqbal has been found guilty of 100 murders. The sentence is that he should be strangled 100 times ... His body should be cut into 100 pieces and put in acid—as he did with his victims ... You will be strangled to death in front of the parents whose children you killed.'

Shahzad Sajid was also sentenced to death. Zafar Ahmed and Mohammad Shabir were sentenced to life, which in Pakistan actually means life.

Iqbal said: 'I am Javed Iqbal, killer of 100 children ... I hate this world, I am not ashamed of my actions and I am ready to die. I have no regrets. I killed 100 children.'

A week later the Council of Islamic Ideology said that cutting up Iqbal's body was contrary to Islam's teaching of respect for the body.

The case went to appeal. The Supreme Court referred it to the local Islamic Court, the Shari'a.

Four days before they were to hand down their decision the question became moot. On 8 October 2001, Javed Iqbal, 43 and Shahzad Sajid, 20, were found beaten and strangled to death by bed sheets in their cells.

Apparently no one heard anything. Autopsies revealed that the men had been bleeding from the mouth and the nose when they died. Prison official Abdussattar Ajiz said that their guard, Iftikar Husain, reported being 'asleep' at the time of the pair's death. Husain did not immediately report the incident, but when he found the bodies he 'untied the knots of the bed sheets, laid the bodies on the floor to create the impression that they were asleep. He did so to save his own skin.' Husain's relief, Liaquat Ali, didn't even bother to check on the prisoners.

Prison officials ruled the deaths a 'suicide'.

Over 5000 prisoners await execution in Pakistan. One wonders how many of them will 'commit suicide'.

2001

Collateral Damage: Timothy McVeigh

Until September 11, 2001, the worst act of terrorism on American soil was the bombing of the Alfred P Murrah Federal Building in Oklahoma City on 19 April 1995. It was all the more shocking to the American public because the bomber wasn't a Muslim fundamentalist or a communist extremist. He was in fact a home-grown, survivalist racist.

The first prisoner to be executed by the American federal authorities since the 15 March 1963 hanging of kidnapper Victor Fuguer, Timothy McVeigh was born in Pendleton, near Buffalo, New York, on 23 April 1968. He was the middle child and only son of Bill and Mickey McVeigh, but it was his grandfather, Eddie McVeigh, who taught him to love guns.

He enlisted in the army in May 1988, where he met fellow survivalist, racist and gun nut, Terry Nichols, during basic training. Nichols left the army after a few months, after obtaining a hardship discharge to raise his son. Nichols married a Filipina, Marife Torres, and they moved in with Nichol's brother, James, on his farm in Michigan. McVeigh stayed on in the army, serving in the 1991 Gulf War, for which he received the Bronze Star, other medals and commendations. However, he left later that year when he failed to make the grade for the Green Berets. Back in the States he worked as a security guard in upstate New York, while frequently visiting Nichols' family. When Federal authorities destroyed David Koresh's Branch Davidian headquarters in Waco, Texas on 19 April 1993, McVeigh was there, watching from the sidelines. Both he and Nichols interpreted the storming of the compound as a fundamental assault on the civil liberties of American citizens and they decided that the government would have to pay for this and any number of other 'anti-libertarian' crimes.

The fictional bombing of the FBI Building in Washington—in a book called *The Turner Diaries* by 'Andrew McDonald' (actually Dr William Pierce, founder of the white-supremacist National Alliance)—inspired McVeigh and Nichol's.

By September 1994, Nichols, under an alias, began to rent storage units throughout the Midwest. Nichols sent his wife to the Philippines while he and McVeigh started stockpiling ammonium nitrate fertiliser, nitromethane racing fuel and diesel. They also stole detonation materials to construct homemade bombs.

The FBI later alleged that Nichols robbed gun-dealer Roger Moore (Nichols denies this and has stated that Moore gave him the cash, valuables and guns). Nichols then went to Texas, taking the goods to his ex-wife, Lana, and her new husband, Leonard Padilla. While staying with the Padillas, Nichols allegedly robbed them of their cash and valuables and placed all the goods in storage outside Las Vegas, leaving the guns for McVeigh. He left a note to Lana 'for the purpose of my death' if he failed to return from the Philippines by 28 January 1995. He also left a note for McVeigh stating 'go for it ... as far as heat, none that I am aware of'.

Nichols then left for the Philippines. When he returned in late January 1995, he discovered that Lana had opened his letters and taken the money he'd left behind. She returned most of it when Nichols demanded it back. McVeigh and Nichols then began to collect their various stockpiles. Nichols decided that he wanted no involvement on the actual day of the bombing and McVeigh agreed. McVeigh and Nichols then separated, but joined up again in mid-April to finalise their bombing plans. They cased the Murrah Building on Easter Sunday, 16 April. McVeigh later stated that he and Nichols started assembling the bombs in Kansas State Park on 18 April, although Nichols denied this.

The next day, 19 April 1995—the second anniversary of end of the Waco siege—McVeigh lit fuses he'd set up in his yellow Ryder Rental truck as he neared the Murrah building. He parked in the front of the building ... then McVeigh walked away.

His 5000 pound (2.3 tonnes) bomb detonated at 9:02 am and tore the Murrah building apart. By that time McVeigh was several blocks away, wearing earplugs.

In the explosion 168 people died, 19 of them children. More than 500 other people were injured, all of them 'collateral damage' according to McVeigh. Later a rescue worker died when a huge chunk of concrete crushed him. One woman, Dana Bradley, could only be saved by having her leg amputated. Her two children and her mother also died that day.

Nichols had stayed home. This fact at least saved Nichols from Death Row when, at the later trial, the jury could not agree that he had helped build the bombs.

Minutes after the bombing McViegh was racing towards central Kansas on Interstate 35, in a yellow 1977 Mercury Grand Marquis with no licence plates, when Oklahoma Highway Patrolman Charles Hanger pulled him over for speeding. While McVeigh was in jail, awaiting trial for these minor charges, psychological profiler Clinton R Van Zandt—who had worked at Waco—predicted that the bomber would be a white male in his twenties with a military record. Identifiable fragments of the Ryder truck were traced to its renter, 'Robert Kling'. Lea McGown, manager of the Dreamland Motel, said she recognised the police portrait of Kling. He was registered at the Dreamland as Timothy McVeigh. The FBI quickly connected McVeigh and Nichols. Nichols soon gave himself up at the police station in Herington, Kansas after the media broadcast his face and name.

FBI searches of Nichols' house uncovered explosive materials and the guns from the Moore 'robbery'.

While on remand, Nichols and McVeigh shared a cellblock at the ADX Prison in Florence, Colorado, America's toughest 'Supermax' prison, also home to the Unabomber, Theodore Kaczynski (serving four life sentences plus 30 years). While there Nichols refused to speak to McVeigh.

McVeigh always maintained that the bombing was a 'legit tactic' to teach the American government a lesson: 'I did it for the larger good.' He also said he was disappointed that the building had not been levelled and later wrote: 'Sorry these people had to lose their lives. But that's the nature of the beast. It's understood going in what the human toll will be.'

On 2 June 1997 a United States District Court convicted McVeigh for the murder of the eight federal employees who died in the Murrah. On 13 June he received the death penalty. Authorities in Oklahoma did not pursue the state trial against McVeigh for the other 161 deaths.

Frances Cummins, widow of bomb victim Richard, made eye contact with McVeigh at his trial. She said: 'He's got a look of death in his eye. It just pierces you. He has no emotions.'

The McVeigh execution attracted worldwide attention: 1400 members of the media were given access when Attorney General John Ashcroft authorised a feed-encrypted, closed-circuit broadcast of McVeigh's execution. Authorities installed a camera above McVeigh's bed in the ceiling of his death chamber. As he lay down to die in Terre Haute, he looked straight at the camera, his face filling a screen more than 600 miles (970km) away in Oklahoma City as 232 survivors and victims' relatives also looked on.

Frances Cummins, who was also there said, he 'never took his eyes off that camera ... the one thing we fear is having that image in our eyes for a long time.'

Two bombing survivors and eight others who lost family members were among the 24 witnesses of McVeigh's execution at Terre Haute. One of them, Paul Howell, father of victim, Karan, said: 'What I was hoping for—and I'm sure most of us were—we could see some kind of maybe, "I'm sorry", you know, something like that. We didn't get anything from his face.'

Another Terre Haute witness, Sue Ashford, said: 'He didn't suffer at all ... the man just went to sleep or, as I said, the monster did. I think they should have done the same thing to him as he did in Oklahoma.'

President George Bush declared that McVeigh 'met the fate he chose for himself six years ago.'

There were no last words; instead McVeigh gave authorities a handwritten copy of William Earnest Henley's 1875 poem:, *Invictus*. It's last words are famous: 'I am the master of my fate; I am the captain of my soul.'

His final meal was a litre of Ben and Jerry's Mint Chocolate Chip Ice Cream. McVeigh, executed by lethal injection on 11 June 2001, was pronounced dead at 8:14 am EDT at the US Federal Penitentiary in Terre Haute, Indiana.

His body was cremated without prior autopsy at a local funeral home. One of his attorneys took his ashes.

A plaque marking his execution was installed at the museum dedicated to his victims within an hour of his death.

***

On 18 November 2003 suspected arsonists burned the CANDLES *Holocaust Museum* in Terre Haute Indiana. Supporters rebuilt the museum and it reopened in April 2005. Although, to date, the arsonists have not been found, on the night of the fire they left a spray-painted message on the outside of the building: 'Remember Timmy McVeigh.'

Terry Nichols remains at ADX Florence and is serving 161 consecutive terms for first-degree murder and eight counts of manslaughter.

2002

The Highway Hooker: Aileen Wuornos

Aileen Carol Wuornos was not 'America's first female serial killer', but she was the first to fit the FBI's definition of one. Previous female serial killers had hit close to home, killing people who they knew or who were in their care. Aileen was the first woman known to have killed multiple strangers.

Aileen Pittman was born on 29 February 1956 in Rochester, Michigan. The woman who became the famous subject of several books, an opera—*Wuornos* (2001), a television movie—*Overkill: The Aileen Wuornos Story* (1992), a film—*Monster* (2003) and documentaries—*Aileen: The Selling of a Serial Killer* (1992) and Aileen: *The Life and Death of a Serial Killer* (2004), also used the names: Sandra Ketsch, Lee Blahovec, Lori Grody and Cammie Marsh Greene. She was always best known as Lee.

Her teenage parents separated before she was even born. Her mother, Diane Pratt, left Lee and her older brother, Keith, in the care of her Finnish grandparents, Lauri and Britta Wuornos, who legally adopted them, although there is a rumour that Lauri was in fact Lee's biological father. Lee was only six years old at the time.

Her father, Leo Pittman, never knew Lee. In 1969 he hung himself in jail while serving time for sodomising an eight-year-old boy. On 23 March 1971, 15-year-old Lee gave birth to a son. The father may have been her brother, Keith, although he could have been the neighbourhood paedophile, a man known locally as 'Chief' who later also committed suicide. After their grandmother's death in July 1971, Lee and Keith became wards of the court. The state didn't do a very good job. Lee spent over a year living in the woods near her former home, giving blow jobs to boys in exchange for cigarettes and just to keep warm.

Lee started working as a prostitute and was jailed in 1974 for disorderly conduct, drunk driving and firing a pistol from a moving vehicle. On 13 July 1976 she was arrested for assault and later paid a US$105 fine. On 17 July 1976 Keith died of throat cancer and Lauri committed suicide shortly after. Lee promptly squandered the US$10 000 life insurance payout. Broke within two months, she moved to Florida.

Run-ins with the law continued. Between 4 May 1982 and 30 June 1983, Lee served 13 months in prison for armed robbery. She was arrested in 1984 for trying to pass forged cheques, named as a suspect in the theft of a pistol in 1985, then cited for driving without a licence. In 1986 she was again arrested for auto theft. On 2 June 1986, Volusia county officers detained Lee after a 'male companion' accused her of pulling a gun on him and demanding $200. A week later she copped a speeding ticket.

Soon afterwards she met lesbian prostitute, Tyria Moore, and the two women became lovers for about a year, although they remained close over the next four years while Lee's behaviour became increasingly strange and erratic. Lee sent threatening letters to a circuit court clerk, vandalised the apartment where she and Tyria lived and made threatening calls to a supermarket while continuing to make a meagre living as a prostitute, soliciting tricks from truck drivers on highways.

13 December 1989

The fully-dressed corpse of Richard Mallory, 51, a Palm Harbour electrician, was found in the woods north west of Daytona Beach. He'd been shot three times in the chest with a .22 pistol.

1 June 1990

The body of David Spears was found in woods 65 kilometres north of Tampa, Florida. He'd been shot six times with a .22 pistol.

6 June

The body of 40-year-old Charles Carskaddon was found about 30 kilometres from where David Spears had been found. Carskaddon had been shot nine times with a .22 pistol.

4 July

The dumped and wrecked car of ex-merchant seaman turned missionary, 65-year-old Peter Siems, was found in Orange Springs. Investigators successfully uncovered a palm print from the car's trunk. Peter Siems' body was never found.

4 August

The body of Eugene Burress, 50, was found in the Ocala National forest. He'd been shot twice, in the back and in the chest with a .22.

12 September

The body of Dick Humphreys, 56, was found, shot seven times with a .22.

19 November

60-year-old trucker Walter Antonio's body, nude except for his socks, was found in woods north west of Cross City 19. He'd been shot three times in the back, and once in the head with a .22.

In each case cash was missing as well as some personal items. The men's vehicles were always found abandoned elsewhere.

Media pressure forced the authorities to show the public identikits of the suspects, believed to be two women. Fingerprint cross-matches and tracing hotel receipts helped to narrow the search, but the clincher came when 'Cammie Greene' pawned Richard Mallory's camera, David Spear's tools and Walter Antonio's ring.

Authorities finally arrested 'Lorie Grody' on outstanding warrants on 9 February 1991 at the Last Resort Bar in Harbour Oaks, Florida. Tyria Moore was traced to her sister's house and agreed to help police in exchange for an immunity deal. Through a series of set-up phone calls

Tyria begged Lee to confess. Finally, on 16 January 1991 she confessed to six killings, refusing to confess to the murder of Peter Siems. She claimed in each case:

> 'I shot 'em 'cause to me it was like a self-defending thing … because I felt if I didn't shoot 'em and I didn't kill 'em, first of all … if they survived, my ass would be gettin' in trouble for attempted murder, so I'm up shit's creek on that one anyway, and if I didn't kill 'em, you know, of course, I had to kill 'em ... or, it's like retaliation, too. It's like: You bastards, you were going to hurt me.'

Within weeks of her arrest both she and the men who arrested her had sold the movie rights to her story, a revelation that, rather hypocritically, shocked the American public.

On 27 January 1991 the jury took 90 minutes to find Lee guilty of the murder of Richard Mallory. She pleaded no contest to the five other murders (not counting Peter Siems).

By 1993 she had received a total of six death sentences: 'How many times you gotta kill me? Know what I mean?'

She spent ten years on Death Row. Originally—for some who bought Lee's 'self-defending' argument—she became a symbol of the injustice that women experience at the hands of a male-dominated legal system. Arlene Pralle, a born-again Christian who claimed God had called upon her to help Aileen, went so far as to legally adopt her. That didn't prevent her from colluding with Aileen's first attorney to secure a movie deal and sell interview rights.

As time wore on Aileen changed her story, maintaining that she had killed the men because she hated them.

Florida Governor Jeb Bush, brother of President George, ordered a psychiatric examination, which found her mentally competent, in marked contrast to the documentaries, which portray her as mentally disturbed.

'I'll be up in Heaven while you all rot in Hell'.

***

At her final media interview with Nick Broomfield she changed her story again, maintaining her innocence. 'A raped woman got executed and was used for books and movies and shit', she said.

The 'Highway Hooker' was executed by lethal injection in Florida State prison on 9 October 2002. She was the third woman to be executed in Florida. A freed slave named Celia was hanged in 1848 and husband and son killer, Judy Buenoano, was electrocuted on 30 March 1998.

Lee's last meal was fried chicken and her last words were: 'I'd just like to say I'm sailing with the rock and I'll be back like Independence Day, with Jesus, 6 June. Like the movie, big mother ship and all, I'll be back.'

Her best friend, Dawn Botkins, scattered Lee's ashes on the grounds of her farm in Michigan.

2004

The Red Hammer: Xang Xinhai

China has the second highest prison population in the world, second only to America. This is surprising, considering that China's population is over four times that of the USA, but with an imprisonment rate almost the same as Australia's, at around 117 per 100 000 of population, you're about six times less likely to be imprisoned in China than in America.

One reason that China's rate is so low is that a veil of secrecy still hangs over a lot of what goes on there, so information is often sparse and questionable. This secrecy has other disadvantages. Authorities often do not give information to the media. This gives the public little knowledge of what danger they might be in, grieving relatives little idea of what progress, if any, the police are making and the general public little opportunity to be on the alert or to inform the police if they see something suspicious.

Another reason that there are comparatively few in Chinese prisons is that justice in China is fast. Prisoners condemned to death don't languish for years on Death Row. The contrast to the situation in America could hardly be greater.

Yang Zhiya—aliases Yang Liu and Yang Xinhai—drifter, itinerant worker and China's most prolific serial killer in recent history, was condemned to death after a 'closed-door' trial lasting only one hour.

His parents—among the poorest farmers from a village of 2000 people in Zhengyang County, Henan—described their youngest of four as 'promising but introverted'. He left home at 17, while still in high school. His father had only seen him twice since.

Some have speculated that he merely killed for the fun of it, although he was released from a labour camp in which he'd been serving time for rape and burglary in 1999. When his girlfriend found out about his time in prison she dumped him. As far as we know, that's when the killings began.

Over four years, travelling on a bicycle, Yang killed on 26 separate occasions, throughout rural areas in the provinces of Shandong, Anhui, Henan and Heibei, all in the north east of China.

His weapons of choice included axes, meat cleavers, shovels and hammers. He entered houses at night, murdering the occupants in their sleep. Neighbours would usually find the bodies. On at least two occasions he killed entire families. In August 2003 he killed a family of five in Heibei.

Later he was also convicted of 23 rapes committed at the murder scenes.

He made some attempts to put the police off the scent. He was always changing clothes and he wore shoes two sizes too big. Yang also reputedly wore white gloves when he killed, often discarding them at the scene of the crime.

Out of all the attacks, only five people managed to escape him.

In the end he was only caught because the police were on the alert for another man. That killer lured at least 17 boys from entertainment venues in the province of Henan, taking them to his house, torturing and strangling them. The Henan man was caught when a boy he was preparing to kill managed to escape. While conducting an inspection of Internet cafes and video-game parlours in the city of Cangzhou, in Heibei, on 3 November 2003, authorities arrested Yang, who was seen 'acting suspiciously'.

When police were able to match his DNA to several crime scenes Yang confessed. Yang himself offered no explanation for his crimes.

China's *Central Television* broadcast an interview after his trial. He said: 'When I killed people I had a desire ... This inspired me to kill more ... I don't care whether they deserved to live or not. It is none of my concern ... I have no desire to be part of society. Society is not my concern.'

On 1 February 2004 in the city of Luohe Hunan, the presiding judge, Yang Qingjiu, convicted Yang Xinhai of the murder of 67 people and sentenced him to death.

Yang waived his right to an appeal.

In Luohe, less than two weeks later on 14 February 2004, he was executed by a shot to the head. He was 38 years old.

China Daily reported that 'Yang told police during interrogation that he hoped to have a chance to live, but if not, he would like to donate his organs'.

His body was cremated.

Cruel and Unusual Punishment

1960–1999

Cruel and Unusual Punishment

America is by no means united in its sentiments about the death penalty. Capital punishment has always been controversial although, depending on who you talk to and which opinion polls you pay attention to, the 'ultimate penalty' has waxed and waned considerably in popularity since the first known judicial execution when Captain George Kendall was shot by firing squad in Jamestown in the colony of Virginia in December, 1607, for 'sowing discord and mutiny'.

The Bureau of Justice Statistics began compiling accurate records from 1930. From that year until 1967, 3859 people were executed under civil jurisdiction in America. Of those executed 54 per cent were black, 45 per cent white and the remaining one per cent 'other.' Of the total during those years, 3827 were men and 35 were women. The peak year was 1935 with 199 executions. The popularity of the death penalty erratically declined over the next 30-odd years and the issue was not without its share of drama.

1960: Caryl Chessman

Caryl Chessman was born on 27 May 1921 and grew up to be a petty hoodlum, armed robber and by his own admission 'not generally regarded as a pleasant or socially minded fellow.' Yet, it was a crime that occurred a couple of months before his eleventh birthday—to which he had no connection—that would seal his fate almost 39 years later.

Between 8 and 10 pm on 1 March 1932, 20-month-old Charles Augustus Lindbergh Jr, the firstborn son of famed aviator Charles Lindbergh and his wife Anne, was kidnapped from his bedroom. William Allen stumbled across the boy's remains 72 days later, on 12 May 1932, in woods only a few blocks from the Lindbergh house. In this famous case a combination of dedicated police work and brilliant forensic science brought German immigrant Bruno Richard Hauptmann to trial and execution for the crime.

On 17 June 1932, the American government passed the 'Lindbergh Law', which made kidnapping a federal offence if the victim crossed a state line or if the kidnapper used the postal service to make ransom demands. In 1933, California passed the 'Little Lindbergh' law. It made any case of kidnapping that involved bodily harm punishable either by life imprisonment without possibility of parole or by the death sentence.

Fast forward to San Francisco in the 1940s. No one knew who the Red Light Bandit was but his modus operandi was well known to his victims. Typically a couple parked in one of the city's many isolated 'lovers lanes' would see a car with a red light flashing approaching them. A man posing as a police officer would get out of the car and begin to question them. The phoney interrogation would rapidly degenerate into assault and robbery of the man. The bandit would then force the woman into his own car where he would either rape her, compel her to perform fellatio on him or both.

Paroled from Folsom Prison—after serving time for one of a countless string of offences—Chessman was free for only a little while when, in January 1948, he was involved in an 80mph (130kmh) car chase in Los Angeles, which ended in a shootout. Chessman was almost killed when a police bullet grazed his head and, when he was arrested, the police decided he was the long sought-after Red Light Bandit.

Chessman claimed he was forced to sign a confession under duress.

From the beginning, the 1949 trial was highly controversial. Chessman chose to represent himself. In his life he had 'developed the habit of doing my own fighting.' He summed up his independence in a famous remark: 'My soul is not for sale.'

He was smart and knowledgeable, but also rough and crude and the jury wasn't impressed. Many have argued that Chessman's abrupt and confrontational manner did nothing to further his case. Facts didn't seem to matter. Chessman did not match any physical descriptions of the Red Light Bandit as reported by witnesses and the two principal female victims of assault at the trial failed to identify Chessman in a line-up. Nevertheless, the jury found Chessman guilty on 17 counts, ranging from robbery to kidnapping and, under the Little Lindbergh law, forcing the women from one car to another constituted kidnapping. The jury did not recommend mercy and Chessman received two death penalties for kidnapping and eight five-year sentences for the robberies.

For the next 12 years Chessman literally fought for his life.

He was unlucky. The court stenographer at his trial died before a third of the proceedings had been transcribed. The remaining transcription fell into the hands of a chronic alcoholic who was also a relative of the prosecutor.

Chessman appealed his conviction on the grounds that the transcripts of his trial were incomplete or incorrect. The Supreme Court ordered the State of California to conduct a full review. Perhaps unsurprisingly, the review found that the transcripts were substantially accurate.

It was not in the courtroom, however, but in prison that Chessman truly found his voice. From San Quentin Prison Chessman completed his first book: Cell 2455 Death Row in 1954. It was a hit, selling half a million copies and translated into 18 languages. From the start Chessman never claimed to be an angel. In his first book he implies that he once killed a man, a murder for which he was never charged or convicted. His argument was always that he was innocent of the charge for which he would be ultimately executed.

After the success of *Cell 2455*, authorities refused to allow him to write anything else except correspondence with his lawyers about his case. Nevertheless, with astounding persistence and almost superhuman tenacity, he continued writing. He worked throughout the night, writing a first draft in longhand, transcribing in shorthand then shredding and flushing the longhand copy down the toilet. He hid the shorthand among legal notations to get the work past prison authorities. He was lucky if he got four hours' sleep a night. He wrote *Trial by Ordeal* this way and published it in 1955.

In *The Face of Justice*, published in 1957, he wrote: 'I won the dubious distinction of having existed longer under death sentence than any other condemned man in the nation's then 179-year history. Day after day, I would go on breaking my own record.' Chessman stated that he knew the true identity of the Red Light Bandit (or perhaps, bandits) but he refused to talk in order to protect people he loved—people he claimed were being threatened. He arranged for proof of the Red Light Bandit's identity to be released 50 years later, sometime around the year 2007, by which time he felt, threats would have become meaningless.

Chessman also published a novel, *The Kid Was a Killer*, in 1960, the year of his death. All four books are now out of print.

The Chessman case became world-famous. Among the people who wrote to the authorities on his behalf were such notables as Eleanor Roosevelt, Aldous Huxley, Ray Bradbury, Norman Mailer and Billy Graham. California Governor Edmund G Brown—although an opponent of capital punishment—was powerless to commute Chessman's sentences. Under the California Constitution, he needed the State Supreme Court's approval and the Court wasn't budging.

To the very end Chessman maintained his innocence, but the years took their toll: 'My once bright dreams of a decent, creative future are maggot-infested … My mirror tells me I am old and aged beyond my 35 years. The fatigue I feel is bone deep. I have an ulcer and tonight it feels as though a hungry rat is gnawing at my duodenum. I fear for my continuing sanity.' It couldn't have helped matters that, by the time of his execution, California had repealed the Little Lindbergh Law and kidnapping no longer carried the death penalty.

After a record eight stays of execution Chessman ran out of time. Just before he entered the gas chamber his last words were: 'I specifically state I was not the Red Light Bandit.'

The Gas Chamber

The California gas chamber at San Quentin is an octagonal metal box, six feet (1.8m) across and eight feet (2.4m) tall, painted a pale green. It was constructed in 1938. A rubber-sealed steel door encloses the chamber, which contains two identical metal chairs. The last time both chairs were used was for a double execution in 1962. The condemned is strapped to a chair and a long stethoscope attached to the chest, so that a doctor can monitor the heartbeat. A bucket filled with dilute sulphuric acid is placed beneath the chair. Suspended above the bucket is a gauze bag filled with sodium cyanide pellets. Once the door is sealed, the executioner pulls a lever releasing the pellets into the bucket. The chemical reaction, between the pellets and the acid, releases hydrogen cyanide gas, which quickly envelops the prisoner.

On the day of Chessman's death, his lawyer, George Davis, made a heroic effort to obtain one final stay of execution. At one minute to 10 the District Court Judge granted the stay and instructed his secretary to call the prison. She misdialled the first time, but reached the warden on the second attempt. By then it was too late. The pellets had already been dropped.

Death by gas requires the condemned prisoner's active participation. They don't always give it. Many have held their breath trying to cling to the final few seconds of life. As former San Quentin warden, Clifton Duffy, described it: 'At first there is evidence of extreme horror, pain, and strangling. The eyes pop. The skin turns purple and the victim begins to drool.' Author Richard Clark of the Capital Punishment UK Website and Dr Richard Traystman from John Hopkins University explain:

> 'The person exposed to this gas remains conscious for a period of time, in some cases for several minutes, again depending on the rate and volume of the gas that is inhaled. During this time, the person is unquestionably experiencing pain and extreme anxiety. The pain begins immediately and is felt in the arms, shoulders, back and chest. The sensation is similar to the pain felt

> by a person during a heart attack where, essentially, the heart is being deprived of oxygen. The severity of the pain varies directly with the diminishing oxygen reaching the tissues.
>
> The agitation and anxiety a person experiences in the hypoxic state will stimulate the autonomic nervous system. (The person) may begin to drool, urinate, defecate or vomit. There will be a muscular contraction. These responses can occur both while the person is conscious or when he becomes unconscious.
>
> When (oxygen deprivation) sets in, the brain remains alive for from two to five minutes. The heart will continue to beat for a period of time after that, perhaps five to seven minutes or longer, though at a very low cardiac output. Death can occur ten to twelve minutes after the gas is released in the chamber … We would not use asphyxiation—by cyanide gas or by any other substance—in our laboratory to kill animals that have been used in experiments.'

After 11 years, 10 months and one week on Death Row, at 10:03 on the morning of 2 May 1960, sixty witnesses watched Chessman die. They reported that he smiled as he inhaled the hydrocyanic gas, but then started nodding to signal that he was in pain. The presiding doctor pronounced Chessman dead at 10:12 am

After death an exhaust fan pumped out excess gas through the chamber's 38-foot-long (11.5m) chimney. Chessman's body was then sprayed with ammonia to neutralise any residual cyanide. Half an hour later orderlies wearing gas masks, protective clothing and rubber gloves removed the body.

Harry Truman responded to the huge international outrage of the Chessman execution saying the outcry was 'a lot of hooey stirred up to keep your mind off what's happening.'

In his last written message Chessman wrote: 'Now that the State has had its vengeance, I should like to ask the world to consider what has been gained.'

The 1955 film '*Cell 2455, Death Row*' and a 1958 Brazilian TV series, *Cela da Morte* were based on Caryl Chessman's book *Cell 2455, Death Row*.

A television film about his life was made in 1977, starring Alan Alda.

With heavy irony, writer Alan Bisbort made the point that professional basketball player Ruben Patterson was convicted of attempted rape in May 2001. Paterson received a suspended sentence of 15 days house arrest and a five-game suspension by the National Basketball Association. In August 2001 he signed a US$33.8 million contract with the Portland Trail Blazers. 'I'm no rapist,' said Paterson 'I'm a great guy.' If you think about the Mike Tyson case as well, it's amazing how times have changed.

★★★

Only Arizona, Maryland and Wyoming still have the gas chamber on their books, all have lethal injection as an alternative method and the gas chamber at the old State Prison in Rawlins, Wyoming, is in fact no longer usable. The most recent criminal to die in a gas chamber in America was Walter LaGrand, in Arizona, on 3 March 1999.

★★★

Chessman is little remembered today, but some have argued that his case went a long way to changing the way the public felt about the death penalty during the 1960s. In 1967, in response to an ever-increasing number of legal challenges, there was an effective moratorium on executions.

In 1972 the Supreme Court in *Thurman v Georgia* 408 US 153 (1972) voted 5–4 that the many wide and varied state laws authorising the death penalty were 'arbitrary and capricious' and constituted cruel and unusual punishment, in violation of the Eighth Amendment to the US Constitution and the 'due process of law' guarantees of the 14th Amendment. The later cases of *Woodson v North Carolina* 428 US 280 (1976) and *Roberts v Louisiana* 428 US 325 (1976) ruled mandatory death penalties unconstitutional.

The states fought back with considerable speed and drafted new laws reflective of Supreme Court rulings. The tide of public opinion and the machinations of lawmakers brought the death penalty back. The *Gregg v Georgia* 428 US 153 (1976) decision upheld the new state laws under the model of 'guided discretion.'

Whatever cases like Caryl Chessman's accomplished was only temporary. The new spirit of the age was born with the execution of Gary Mark Gilmore.

1977: Gary Mark Gilmore

Born Faye Robert Coffman on 4 December 1940 to Frank and Bessie Gilmore, Gary was the second son, following Frank Jr. Renamed Gary by his mother, Gilmore was the classic 'difficult child'. It is highly probable that Gilmore would have become just another one of the thousands of small-time criminals and murderers throughout history who were scarcely worth a mention in the annals of crime: except for two things:

1. Author Norman Mailer decided to immortalise Gilmore in his book *The Executioner's Song*
2. The way Gilmore died or, more accurately, chose to die.

He was highly intelligent, with an IQ later measured at 130, but he was also impulsive and self-indulgent. He started drinking when he was 12, constantly skipped school and drove his teachers and fellow classmates crazy. Gilmore's youngest brother, Mikal, later wrote in his own book, Shot in the Heart, that their father Frank was an alcoholic and a professional conman with a habit of regularly beating his sons for no reason. No matter what they did, they couldn't win. Yet, Frank's perverse idea of love showed when he hired a clever lawyer to keep Gary out of jail after his first arrest. Gilmore, however, was out of control and spent a year at the McLaren Reform School for Boys after he was caught stealing. This was soon followed by several years in an out of jail, until he stole a car and served time at the Oregon State Correctional Institution. He was 20 years old and in jail the day his father died. On hearing the news he became so difficult to handle and so violent that authorities started 'medicating' him with the anti-psychotic drug Prolixin—a treatment that only stopped when Bessie intervened. It seems to be about the only positive thing Gilmore's mother ever did for him. Most of the time, she believed that she was powerless against the influence of an evil spirit that haunted her family.

Out of jail and in again at 21 after a robbery and assault that netted him all of $11, Gilmore served time at Oregon State Penitentiary. While he was there, his younger brother Galen was stabbed in the stomach and died shortly after.

In 1967, after having spent 9½ years of the last 11½ years in jail and on trial for armed robbery Gilmore addressed the court: 'I want freedom and I realise that the only way to get it is to quit breaking the law … I've got problems and if you sentence me to additional time, I'm going to compound them.' The court sentenced him to another nine years in jail anyway. After more violence and several suicide attempts, he started corresponding with his cousin, Brenda Nicol, in Provo, Utah, from a maximum-security penitentiary in Marion, Illinois. Although she hadn't seen Gilmore since he was a child, she felt that all that Gary needed was a chance. He had one when he was paroled in April 1976. Living in Provo with his cousin, Gilmore fell in love with Nicole Baker Barrett and a white Ford ute.

According to Barrett, when Gilmore moved in with her he drank so often and took so many drugs that she just couldn't take the ever-present threat of violence from him and she left him, taking her two children with her. This was more than Gilmore could take.

On Monday 19 July 1976, Gilmore acquired the white Ford ute from the dealer on the understanding that, if he failed to make a single payment, it would be repossessed immediately. Gilmore paid a visit to Nicole's mother and met up with April, Nicole's mentally unstable younger sister. Around 10:30 that night Gilmore left April and the truck and walked round the corner into a self-service petrol station in Orem, Utah. He pulled out a .22 Browning automatic, forced the attendant Max Jensen into the toilet and told him to lie down on the floor. Gilmore shot Jensen in the head: 'This one is for me' then again 'For Nicole.' Blood covered his trousers. He left the station without even taking any money then took April to the cinema to watch *One Flew over the Cuckoo's Nest*. After the movie they went to Brenda's, where Gilmore changed his clothes. He and April left and took a room at a Holiday Inn. At around 11 pm a customer found Max Jensen's body and the hunt was on for his killer.

On Tuesday 20 July Gilmore took the truck to a petrol station near his Uncle Vern's house for a repair that would take 20 minutes. On impulse, Gilmore walked into the City Centre Motel next door. He met the 25-year-old motel manager Ben Bushnell, demanded the motel's cash box, then shot Bushnell on the spot. When Bushnell's pregnant wife, Debbie, appeared Gilmore ran, pocketed the $125 he'd taken, hid the cash box in a bush and walked another block. He attempted to hide his gun, only to accidentally shoot himself in the hand. Gilmore then picked up his truck, but the garage owner, Norman Fulmer, had heard about the hotel shooting and, as Gilmore drove away, Fulmer reported the truck's licence plate to the police.

News spread quickly. Uncle Vern soon realised that his erratic nephew must have somehow been involved. He called his daughter Brenda and, when Gilmore called her, she called the police. They soon closed in on him. Gilmore had been out of jail only three months. In custody in the police station at Orem the next day, Gilmore telephoned Brenda and asked her why she had turned him in. 'You commit a murder Monday and commit a murder Tuesday. I wasn't waiting for Wednesday to roll around,' she said. As Mailer would also recount:

Brenda said, 'Gary, you're going to go down hard this time. You're going to ride this one clear to the bottom.'

> He said, 'Man, how do you know I'm not innocent?'
>
> 'Gary, what's the matter with your head?'
>
> 'I don't know,' Gary said, 'I must have been insane.'
>
> Brenda asked, 'What about your mother? What do you want me to tell her?'
>
> He was quiet for a while. Then he said, 'Tell her it's true.'
>
> Brenda said, 'Okay. Anything else?'
>
> 'Just tell her I love her.'

***

Gilmore's trial began on 5 October 1976 and lasted two days. Inevitably, he was found guilty of the first-degree murder of Ben Bushnell. That was enough, they didn't need to try him for Jensen's death too. Gilmore was scheduled to die on 15 November.

On 2 July 1976, three weeks before Gilmore's murders, Utah had successfully reinstated capital punishment. Utah retained a firing squad as an option for execution because, according to Mormon doctrine, the soul of the murderer could be saved only if their own blood was shed: the principle of blood atonement. According to the law, Gilmore had to be executed within 60 days of sentencing. Yet, Utah had not executed a criminal in 16 years. Attorney General, Earl Dorius, wasn't even sure how to organise a firing squad.

Gilmore didn't want to appeal. He didn't want to spend the rest of his life on Death Row and asked the Utah Supreme Court to uphold his request. They did.

***

Special interest groups were outraged and—over Gilmore's protests—his lawyers filed for appeal anyway and the court granted them a stay of execution. Gilmore was determined to die and he wrote to Nicole. They formed a suicide pact. She managed to smuggle in 50 barbiturates in a balloon, hidden in her vagina. Though they both took their doses, they both survived.

Nicole was sent to a psychiatric facility for observation and she and Gilmore were forbidden further contract. Gilmore protested by starting a hunger strike. He then sold the rights to his story to the American Broadcasting Corporation for US$50 000. When interviewed, he made it quite clear that he wanted to die on 6 December, the next scheduled day for his execution. On 3 December Bessie Gilmore requested a stay for her son. Gilmore published a letter effectively asking her to butt out, but the execution was delayed again and Gilmore tried to commit suicide, again unsuccessfully.

The night before he died, Gilmore was given lots of drugs and was drunk on whisky that Uncle Vern had brought him. Singer Johnny Cash called him and sang him a song. Gilmore tried to sing along. He then taped a request to Nicole that she kill herself for him.

As late as 7:30 am on the morning of 17 January 1977, after more wrangling between the courts, the US Supreme Court finally intervened and ordered the execution to go ahead as scheduled.

Five volunteers made up the firing squad and pointed their .30-30 Winchester model 94 carbines through small square holes in a wall of the execution chamber: a converted prison cannery in Utah State Prison. Only four of the guns were loaded, thus allowing each man the possibility that their gun would not shoot the condemned man. Gilmore broke his watch, set at the time he was scheduled to die, and gave it to Uncle Vern to give to Nicole. A black corduroy hood went on his head, a white paper target over his heart and officials strapped him into a chair that was surrounded by sandbags to catch his blood.

His last words were: 'Let's do it.'

At 8:06 am witnesses heard three distinct shots and watched as Gilmore's head slumped forward into the restraining strap and blood flowed from his heart down his shirt and onto the floor.

His was the first execution in America since 1967. Uncle Vern, Laverne Damico, said that Gilmore 'died like he wanted to die, with dignity. He got his wish.' He was 36 and had spent 18 of the last 21 years of his life in prison.

Gilmore had requested to be an organ donor and within hours of his execution two people received his corneas, a fact that inspired punk band 'The Adverts' top 20 hit: *Gary Gilmore's Eyes.*

His body was cremated and the ashes spread in three parts of Utah.

History has shown an erratic but increasingly fast rise in executions, peaking at 98 in 1999. In 2004, 59 people were executed in America.

The death penalty continues to provoke strong emotions. Consider the case of John Albert Taylor.

1996: John Albert Taylor

Convicted sexual assailant, robber and paedophile John Albert Taylor was visiting his sister in Washington Terrace in Salt Lake City when—on a morning in June 1988—he made his way into another apartment in the same building. There he raped and strangled 11-year-old Charla Nicole King with a telephone cord, then gagged her with a pair of panties.

That afternoon, Sherron King found her daughter—the next day would have been Charla's 12th birthday.

Convicted and sentenced to death on the evidence of fingerprints on the telephone, Taylor also chose to die by Utah's firing squad to make a political point. He wanted to make it difficult for the State and maintained that he did not want lethal injection, because he did not want to 'flop around on the gurney like a dying fish.' He spent the next six years on Death Row involved in the usual series of legal manoeuvres until he eventually decided to drop his appeals. The months leading up to his execution brought tremendous controversy. Senate minority Whip, Ron Allen, said at the time: 'Why do these guys get a choice when their victims didn't? Let's take the choice out of the situation and let's take the unwarranted publicity out of it.' Sherron King poignantly said:

> 'I personally don't think anyone has the right to choose their own death, especially when they have murdered. I think they take that right away from themselves ... People forgot about Charla. They could only see that John was going to die, but the fact is a little girl died viciously at his hands. That is not hate talking, that is truth talking ... It was like my daughter's life meant nothing. He was a master at publicity.'

After a last meal of 'pizzas with everything' Taylor died by gunfire at 12:03 am on 26 January 1996, just over 19 years after Gary Gilmore's execution.

* * *

As if to compound the controversy and bring more attention to the methods of execution, the state of Delaware chipped in with its own contribution.

The day before John Taylor's death Billy Bailey also died.

1996: Billy Bailey

Billy Bailey was born in 1947, his parents' 19th child. His mother died after giving birth to a further five children. Social workers found Bailey at 12 years old, 'a seriously disturbed child who needs professional help' which was hardly surprising given the years of physical and psychological abuse he had suffered at the hands and mouth of his stepmother.

In 1979 Bailey was serving time at Plummer house, a work release facility in Wilmington Delaware, when he escaped and appeared at the home of his foster sister, Sue Ann Cooker, in Cheswold, Delaware.

While running an errand with Charles, Sue Ann's husband, Bailey robbed a package store clerk at gunpoint, then forced Cooker to drop him off near the farm of 80-year-old Gilbert Lambertson and his 73-year-old wife, Clara. High on Valium® and alcohol, he asked for their truck. When they refused to hand it over to him he shot Gilbert twice in the chest with his pistol and once in the head with the Lambertson's own shotgun. He then shot Clara, once in the shoulder with the pistol, once in the abdomen and once in the neck with a shotgun. Both Lambertsons died.

By now, Charles Cooker had alerted police and a police helicopter spotted Bailey as he ran across the Lambertson's farm. Although Bailey took a shot at the helicopter he was soon apprehended.

Why did he do it? 'I don't really know. I just know that I feel bad about it. It hurts sometimes when I think about it. When I say hurt, I think about the Lambertsons and how much they hate me and I start to cry and sometimes I cry myself to sleep at night.'

Convicted in 1980, Bailey was condemned to die. He chose hanging to make his death as difficult as possible for the state and for the added bonus of being potentially embarrassing. In 1986, Delaware introduced lethal injection, but Bailey continued to make his stand for the 16 years he spent on Death Row. In an interview with the *Wilmington News Journal* in 1996 he said 'I didn't choose hanging, the state chose it for me. Asking a man to choose how to die is more barbaric than hanging.'

Bailey was only the third man to hang in America since 1965. As Bailey's was the first hanging in Delaware in 50 years authorities—who were well aware that they could botch the whole execution—had to relearn the art. Edmund Lyons, Bailey's attorney, said: 'It's not as if you can look in the yellow pages under H for hangman.'

Delaware authorities turned to their counterparts in Washington State, who had previously hanged Westley Allan Dodd in 1993 and Charles Campbell in 1994 and to a 1969 manual from the US Army. They learned that the manila hemp rope had to be ¾ of an inch to 1¼ quarter inches in diameter (18mm–30mm). It had to be boiled and pre-stretched to eliminate springing or coiling and had to be lubricated with melted paraffin 'to ensure a smooth gliding action.' They also had to relearn the condemned's height/weight formulas to ensure that the rope would not be too long and cause decapitation, nor too short and cause slow strangulation.

Bailey's first execution date was scheduled for 1986 at the Delaware Correctional Centre at Smyrna and a special gallows had to be built just for him, but between one appeal and another the structure stood for 10 years and had to be renovated and strengthened before it could be used.

49 year-old Bailey spent his last 24 hours in a caravan parked close to the gallows. He slept, ate, watched television and talked to the prison chaplain, his attorney and his sister Betty.

His last meal was a well-done steak, a baked potato with sour cream and butter, buttered rolls, peas and vanilla ice cream.

Minutes before midnight on 24 January 1996 two guards, wearing black jumpsuits and black hoods held in place by baseball caps, led Bailey up the 23 steps to the gallows platform 15 feet (4.5m) above the ground.

Warden and hangman Robert Snider stood on Bailey's right as he stood on the trap. A nylon-webbing strap bound Bailey's ankles together and a black hood now covered his head and upper chest. Snyder then placed the noose around Bailey's head, making sure that the knot was correctly positioned beneath Bailey's left ear. Snyder asked him if he had any last words: 'No, sir.'

At 12:04 am on 25 January 1996, Snyder pulled the lever. The trap door opened with a loud bang and Bailey fell through. At 12:15 am the presiding doctor pronounced him dead.

Delbert Lambertson, 70, his brother Saxon Lambertson, 68, seven reporters and 12 officials witnessed the hanging. Delbert, talking about his role as witness said: 'It's something that I think I'm obligated to do on behalf of my father and mother. That's the way I feel. When we see this happen, I can say to my mom and dad, we finally got him.' Saxon said that his parents ' … were very innocent people. They were old and small and he was a big brute. He chose to shoot them, so he chose to die.'

Only Washington State still allows hanging, although to date, no other official judicial hanging has taken place in America.

***

As for the next least controversial method of excecution, ten American states still have electrocution on their books: Alabama, Arkansas, Florida, Kentucky, Nebraska, South Carolina, Tennessee and Virginia, with Illinois and Oklahoma keeping their options open in case lethal injection is ever ruled unconstitutional. The days of the electric chair may also be numbered. Cases like that of Alan Lee Davis can be a little embarrassing.

1999: Allen Lee 'Tiny' Davis

It was a cruel irony, considering how intimately his company was involved in the history of executions, but Westinghouse Corporation executive, John Weiler was away on a business trip in Pittsburgh when, on 11 May 1982, 37-year-old Davis broke into the house of his neighbours in Jacksonville, Florida.

Davis intended to rape nine-year-old Kristina Weiler and rob the house, but instead attacked Kristina's mother, 37-year-old secretary Nancy Weiler, who was three months pregnant with the family's third child. Davis bludgeoned her with his .357 gun over 25 times—so savagely that the trigger guard, the wooden grips and metal frame of the gun's handle broke. When police found her body she was barely recognisable.

Davis then tied Kristina to a chair and shot her twice in the face. As five-year-old Kathy Weiler tried to run away Davis shot her in the back, beat her and crushed her skull.

The day after would have been Kristina's 10th birthday.

Davis left so much evidence both at and after the crime scene, that his conviction and sentencing was a foregone conclusion.

'Tiny' Davis spent 16 years on Death Row, ballooning to 344 pounds.

His last meal was a lobster tail, fried potatoes, a quarter kilo (1½ pounds)

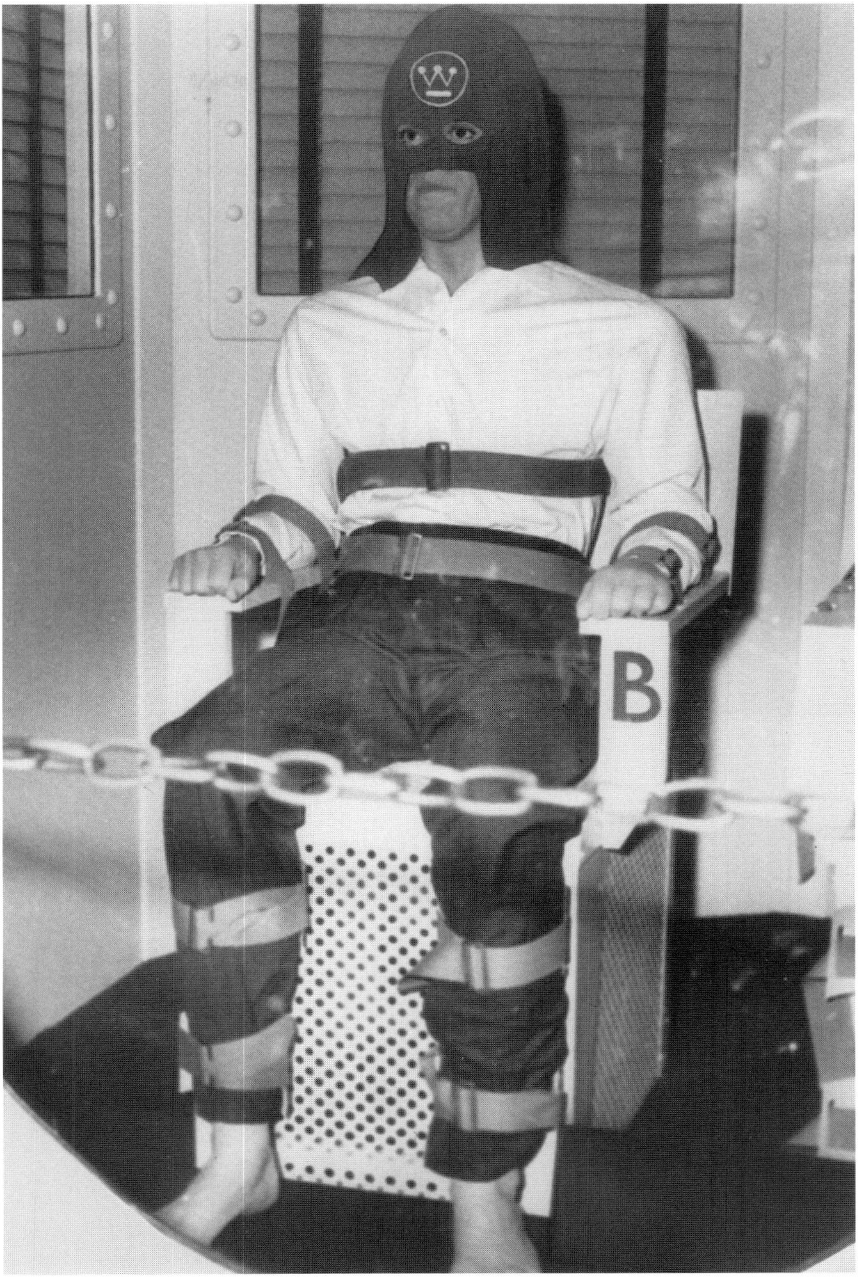

A 1945 photograph of an American prisoner, moments before the gas chamber was sealed for his execution. Note the Westinghouse logo on the hood. Being 'Westinghoused' became the popular term for execution by electric chair, despite the electric generators—for the first execution by electrocution—being supplied by rival company, Edison. *Getty Images*

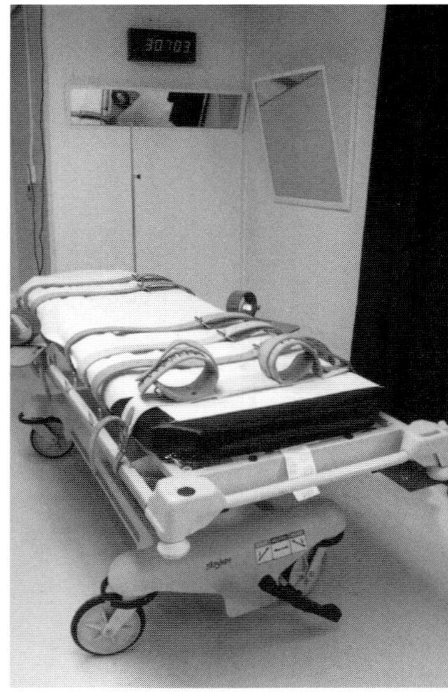

Industrial Execution

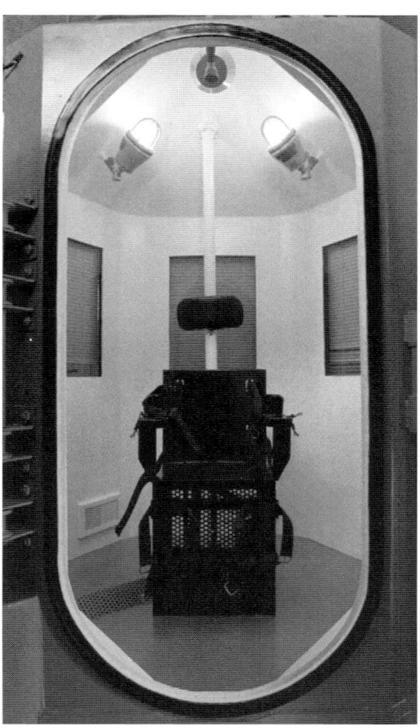

Above left: This new electric chair, made of oak in 1998, replaced 'Ol Sparky', Florida's original chair made in 1923. The wooden structure of the chair is new, but it retains the same original electrical circuits that killed Ted Bundy in 1989. The execution chamber at Florida State Prison, Starke, can now accommodate either the chair or the gurney (above right) and is used for both lethal injections and electrocutions.

Left: The gas chamber at the Florence Prison Complex in Florence, Phoenix, Arizona in 1999. During the execution, cyanide pellets drop into a mixture of water and acid releasing cyanide gas that rises as a blue mist.
The condemned prisoner inhales the gas, experiences symptons similar to a heart attack, suffers cardiac arrest and dies after several minutes of excruciating pain. *AFP/Getty Images*

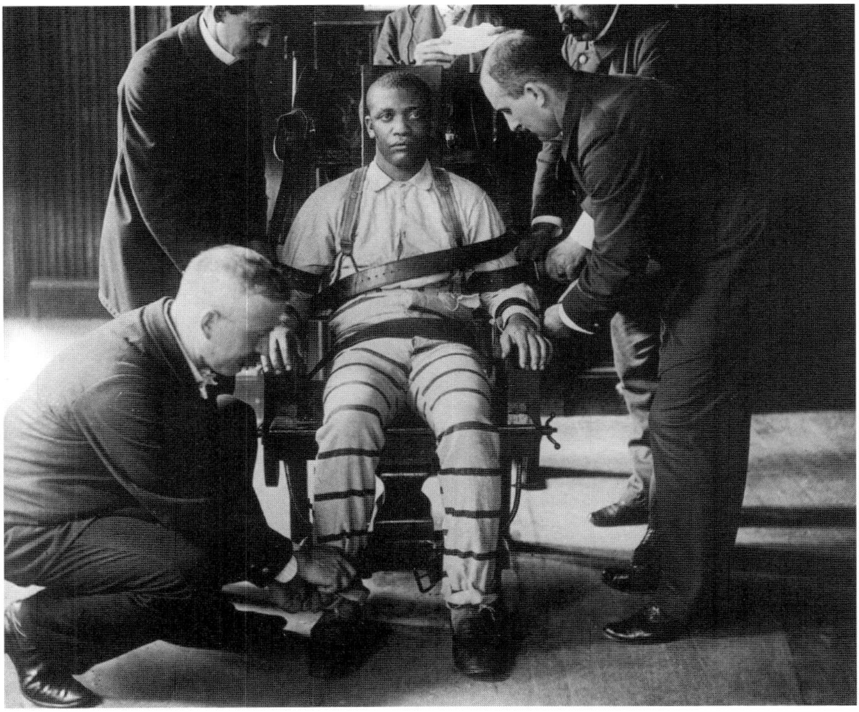

Five white men secure an African-American man to the electric chair in Sing-Sing prison, Ossining, New York, around 1900.
Getty Images

Dr Hawley Harvey Crippen poisoned his wife in London and almost avoided detection, but the stress proved too much for him. *Getty Images*

Ruth Ellis' blonde-bombshell image could hardly have inspired sympathy in a British Jury in the 1950s.
Getty Images

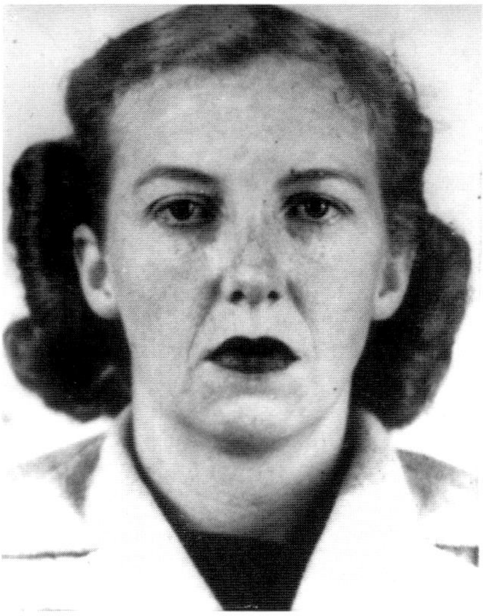

Perth serial killer, Eric Edgar Cooke's tragic life led to a series of senseless deaths, including his own, on the gallows, on 26 October 1964. *Newspix*

Police mug shot of Jean Lee who, on 19 February 1951, was the last woman hanged in Australia. She was so terrified of dying that doctors had to sedate her for the execution. *Newspix*

Ronald Joseph Ryan (left) was the last man hanged in Australia on 3 February 1967 for shooting prison warder, George Hodson, (right). His trial and execution sparked a storm of controversy that remains unresolved to this day. *Newspix.*

Caryl Chessman was a difficult man to like, but the books he wrote while awating execution became best sellers. His eloquence couldn't save him and he died in San Quentin Prison's gas chamber, California, on 2 May 1960. *Getty Images*

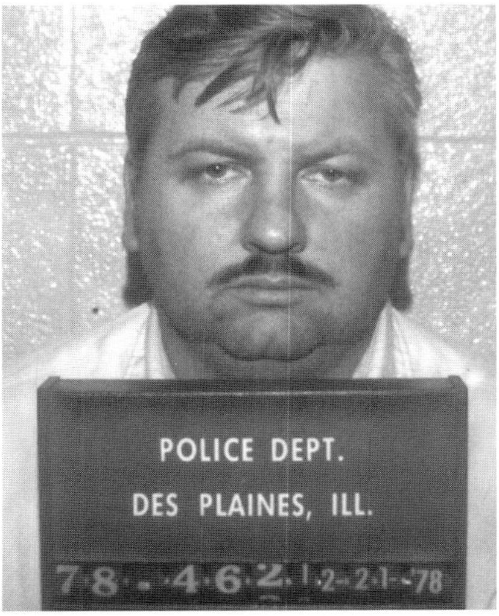

John Wayne Gacy's arrest photo of 21 December 1978. Many of the more than 33 young men he raped and murdered were never identified. *Getty Images*

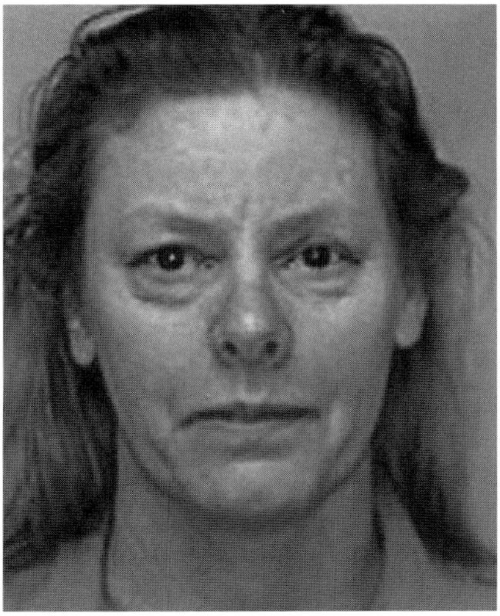

To many Americans Aileen Wuornos was so obviously mentally ill that her execution, by lethal injection, on 9 October 2002, was immoral. *Newspix*

Javed Iqbal murdered at least 100 young boys, but not before he interviewed them and made copious notes about their miserable lives. Javed probably thought he was doing them a favour. *Newspix.*

Stanley 'Tookie Williams' execution on 13 December 2005, raised many questions about the quality of mercy and the value of redemption. *AFP/Newspix*

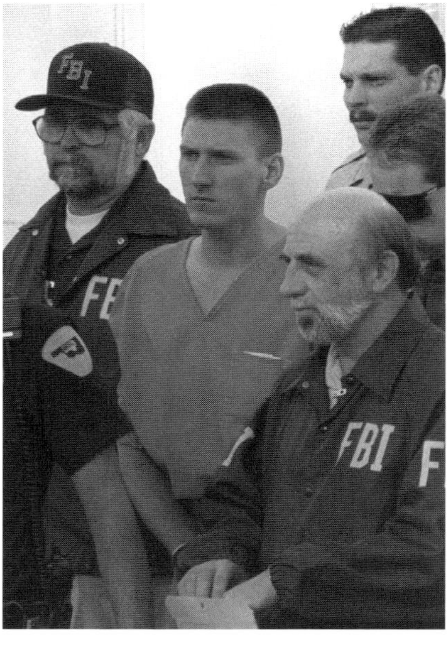

Defiant to the end, Oklahoma Bomber, Timothy McVeigh showed no emotion as he faced the world in America's first televised execution on 11 June 2001. *AFP/Newspix*

Lee Boyd Malvo (left) could have picked a better father figure than Washington Sniper, John Allen Muhammad (right). After a killing spree across America, Malvo was given life and Muhammad the death sentence. Their trials continue. *AFP/Newspix*

Chinese police with a group of criminals, just before their deaths, at an 'execution rally'. Images such as this demonstrate the wide cultural differences and attitudes to the death penalty throughout the world.
The number of executions in China is a state secret, but the Chinese use these rallies to demonstrate that the condemned have lost the right to be considered people. There's something chillingly final about having your name crossed out in red ink.
AFP/Getty Images

It must be difficult for Khoa Nyuyen (left) knowing that your mismanaged life led to the death of your twin brother, Tuong van (right), in a Singapore jail. The Van Nguyen case reminds us that each execution touches the lives of countless others.
Jon Hargest/Newpix.

Myuran Sukumaran, acknowledged leader of the Bali Nine heroin smuggling operation that led to his death sentence and that of cohort, Andrew Chan, by the Denpasar District Court, Bali, Indonesia in February 2006.
AFP/Newspix

of fried shrimp, 200 grams (six ounces) of fried clams strips, half a loaf of garlic bread and a litre (32 ounces) of A&W Root Beer.

On 8 July 1999 at Florida State prison, 54-year-old Davis was strapped into Florida's new electric chair. He became one of those rare individuals who became famous, at least for a short while, not because of his life or his achievements, but because of his death.

Florida had recently completely renovated the execution chamber at the cost of US$42 142. Providing for lethal injections had cost the Department of Corrections approximately $30 000, so for whatever it cost from the leftover $10 000 the new oak chair was comparatively inexpensive. The chair was near replica of Ol' Sparky, the state's 75-year-old veteran that had executed Ted Bundy. In fact, Davis had insisted that Ol' Sparky be replaced.

On 4 May 1990, as Jesse Tafero was being executed, the synthetic sponge lining his skullcap burst into flames and set his head on fire. When the synthetic sponge was replaced with fire resistant, natural sea-sponge this problem disappeared—at least until Pedro Medina's head burst into flames during his execution on 25 March 1997. Aside from these concerns, Davis also claimed that the chair would not be able to take his weight and that the electrical circuitry would adequately account for the electrical resistance of his copious fat tissue. Although the oak structure of *Ol' Sparky Mark II* was new, the electrical apparatus was the same as the old one.

* * *

Davis had no last words.

Assistant Warden Aubrey D Thornton testified that Davis' face began to turn red after a large, wide leather strap was wrapped around his mouth. At least twice Davis made unintelligible sounds, variously described as muffled screams, moans or yells. Justice Leander J Shaw Jr, among others, concluded that Davis was beginning to suffocate at this point. In a later report, Illinois forensic pathologist Robert Kirschner, MD stated that Davis' death was due to at least partial asphyxiation.

After the mouth strap, a skullcap and hood covered Davis' shaved, Electro-Cream-smeared head.

The Department of corrections paid a private citizen $150 to operate the chair. At 7:05 am the chair ran 1500 volts for eight seconds, 600 volts for 22 seconds, and 1500 volts for 4.5 seconds to execute Allen Lee Davis.

Electrocution kills by burning, especially as the current follows the path of nerve tissue, cooking the flesh as it goes. Although the current renders the victim unconscious within milliseconds, violent fits often happen during electrocution, resulting in dislocation and fractures. US Supreme Court Justice William Brenner once described it:

> '... the prisoner's eyeballs sometimes pop out and rest on [his] cheeks. The prisoner often defecates, urinates, and vomits blood and drool. The body turns bright red as its temperature rises, and the prisoner's flesh swells and his skin stretches to the point of breaking. Sometimes the prisoner catches fire ... Witnesses hear a loud and sustained sound like bacon frying, and the sickly sweet smell of burning flesh permeates the chamber.'

After the process examiners usually have to wait for the body to cool down before they can begin their autopsy.

As the current ran through him a spot of blood appeared on Davis' chest and grew slowly until it was some 8 inches (19cm) across. Although prison officials maintained that the blood had come from a nosebleed some witnesses said it seemed to come from Davis' chest. You can look at the pictures taken at the time and judge for yourselves. Witnesses report that Davis' chest did convulse at least twice before prison medical officials declared him dead at 7:15 am.

Civil libertarians were outraged, citing the suffocation, blood and convulsions as evidence of the barbaric nature of the electric chair.

Governor Jeb Bush, brother of President George said: 'Everybody's getting all worked up about a nose bleed.'

John Weiler, who had a front-row-centre seat at the execution of his family's murderer, said: 'It is cruel and unusual punishment of the victims, living and dead, to know that this animal ... still breathes. I've had to wait 17 years for some type of closure to this. No one else should have to do that. Any more than one year to [carry out] a sentence is ridiculous. The execution today was a legal, moral and righteous one, and I can assure you God approves.'

On 2 August 1999, senior Judge Clarence T Johnson found that Florida's use of the electric chair did not constitute cruel and unusual punishment and was therefore not unconstitutional.

***

Changes have continued, although not always in the states that generate the most controversy.

To cite only a few examples among many in recent history: 5 October 2001 Georgia Supreme Court held that the use of the electric chair was cruel and unusual punishment in violation of the State Constitution. In a 4–3 decision the court stated that electrocution 'inflicts purposeless physical violence and needless mutilation that makes no measurable contribution to accepted goals of punishment ... we hold that death by electrocution, with its spectre of excruciating pain and its certainty of cooked brains and blistered bodies, violates the prohibition against cruel and unusual punishment in Article I, Section I, Paragraph XV of the Georgia Constitution.' Justice Leah Ward Sears, now Chief Justice of the Georgia High Court, had also noted earlier that electrocution 'offends the evolving standards of decency that characterise a mature, civilised society.'

Nebraska is the only state where electrocution is the only method of execution. The most recent electrocution in America was of James Tucker, in South Carolina, on 28 May 2004.

On 15 March 2004, Republican Governor Olene Walker signed legislation into law that took full effect on 3 May 2004. The law effectively ended the firing squad as a method of execution in that state. There will be no more Gary Gilmores or John Taylors unless the four prisoners on that State's Death Row who elected the firing squad before the legislation persist in choosing it.

Another law eliminated executions on Sundays, Mondays and public holidays. They save money that way.

Oklahoma and Idaho are now the only places in America that reserve the possibility of execution at gunpoint. However, shooting a criminal remains by far the most popular method of execution in capital cases in the rest of the world: usually a simple shot to the back of the head, more rarely by firing squad, in a cell in the prison or in an isolated field. It depends on where you are. In China, the criminal's family even has to pay for the bullet. In Thailand, 20 miles (32km) outside Bangkok, in Bang Kwang Maximum Security Prison, there is a soundproof room where the single state executioner performs his task with a mounted machine gun or two. The prisoner enters in chains, a white cloth blindfolds him and he has flowers draped on his hands as an offering to Buddha. The executioner fires shots at a target on a canvas screen between the gun and the prisoner. The target is level with the condemned prisoner's heart.

The chamber is called: 'The Place to Relieve Suffering.'

★★★

In America, in spite of all the protests of abolitionists and dramatic gestures such as the decision of Republican Governor George Ryan on 11 January 2003 to commute the death penalty to life imprisonment for all prisoners on Death Row in Illinois, the pendulum shows no sign of swinging back.

For the moment at least, the death penalty is here to stay.

Waiting for Death

On Death Row

The United States is unique among the 'mature economies' in its retention of the death penalty. True to its spirit of democracy and a cultural sense of fair play, it also holds its prisoners for the longest time. Poorer countries simply can't afford to keep their convicted murderers in jail too long. It's cheaper to kill them. Others, such as Singapore, simply want to get it over with. The United States enshrines the right to a fair trial in its constitution. With serious questions about legal proceedings and evidence regularly turning up cases of injustice, America has to be careful about making sure that they've covered all their bases—even if it does mean keeping convicted murderers on Death Row for years and sometimes decades.

The Night Stalker: Richard Ramirez

The man who became the 'Valley Intruder' and 'The Night Stalker' was born Ricardo Leyva Ramirez in El Paso, Texas on 29 February 1960. He was the youngest child of Mercedes and Julian Ramirez.

Many people have speculated about what turned Richard into a monster. Was it the radiation poisoning that his parents had been exposed to? Was it the toxic chemicals that his mother was mixing while she was pregnant with him? His father Julian, a policeman, had a temper. Was it Richard's habit of spending the night at the local cemetery to escape the beatings? Was it the possible abuse by a male teacher? Was it being knocked out cold twice in his childhood? Was it his epilepsy?

Perhaps it was his cousin Mike, the war veteran who often showed Richard pictures of him raping and killing women in Vietnam. Was it the animal hunts Mike took him on? Was it the day that Mike shot his wife in the face, killing her as Richard looked on, the gore spraying his face?

Maybe it was the culture that celebrates violence as a means to power. Maybe it was the petty thefts that Richard committed to support his drug habits: the marijuana, the cocaine, the LSD, the PCP. Maybe it was the Church of Satan he found when he moved to California in 1978.

Maybe it was being arrested in Pasadena in 1981 and again in LA in 1984 for auto theft.

Maybe it was his diet of sugar-laden, junk food and bad hygiene that rotted his teeth, gave him bad skin, his trade-mark foul breath and bad body odour, which left their lasting impressions on the victims who survived. Maybe it was because he listened to AC/DC's record *Highway to Hell* and the song 'Night Prowler' once too often. Who knows?

All that experience at breaking and entering certainly helped when he started killing. The 'tall, dark, gaunt, Hispanic' stranger had one of the simplest methods of all serial killers for finding victims. He just wandered around until he found an open window or an unlocked door: easy during two stiflingly hot summers.

His capture was inevitable. He didn't care about leaving evidence. He often didn't care about leaving victims alive who would remember him. Even if he were caught, Satan would save him.

June 28, 1984

Glassell Park—Jennie Vincow, 79—stabbed repeatedly, raped, beaten, throat slashed so brutally she was almost decapitated—found the next morning by her son, Jack. Police found fingerprints on the windowsill.

February 25, 1985

California—six-year-old girl abducted and raped.

February 20, 1985

Telegraph Hill—sisters Mary, 70, and Christina Caldwell, 50—stabbed to death.

March 11, 1985

California—kidnapped and raped a nine-year-old girl.

March 17, 1985

Rosemead—Maria Hernandez, 20—assaulted but escaped. When Ramirez shot her in her car park Maria instinctively raised her hands to her face. The bullet ricocheted from the keys she was holding. Thinking she was dead, Ramirez entered her apartment and found her flat mate Dayle Okazaki, 34, who he promptly shot at point-blank range. Police found Ramirez's navy blue baseball cap in the garage.

March 17, 1985

Monterey Park—Tsai-Lian (Veronica) Yu, 30—while Veronica was stopped at a red light Ramirez dragged her from her yellow Chevrolet, called her a bitch then shot her at point blank range in her side. As she struggled desperately to escape he shot her three times in the back before getting away. Witnesses called officers Endo and Gorajewski to investigate. They found Veronica and called an ambulance but she died before it arrived.

March 20, 1985

Eagle Rock—8-year-old girl abducted and raped.

March 27, 1985

Monterey Park—Vincent Zazzara, 64 and his wife Maxine, 44—Ramirez shot Vincent through the left temple as the man slept on his sofa. He tied Maxine up with pantyhose while robbing the house. Maxine found the pistol the couple kept under the bed but when she fired, the gun was empty. Vincent had emptied it the week before when children had come to visit and had not reloaded it. Ramirez then shot Maxine in the head and butchered her corpse, slicing her face, gouging out her eyes, cutting her neck, abdomen and genitals, stabbing her left breast in an attempt to cut out her heart, but leaving only a T-shaped wound. Family friend Bruno Polo found them the next morning.

The Zazzara murders established the pattern for Ramirez's style. Put the man out of action as soon as possible, then take your time with the woman and any children.

May 14, 1985

Monterey Park—Bill Doi, 66, and his wife Lillian, 56—Ramirez shot Bill in the mouth, wounding but not killing him. Bill attacked but Ramirez beat him in the head. He then went to invalid Lillian, thumb-cuffed her, robbed the house and raped her over her semi-conscious husband. Bill called 911 but died in hospital. Lillian lived to describe their attacker.

May 29, 1985

Monrovia—Mabel 'Ma Bell' Bell 83, and her invalid sister Florence 'Nettie' Lang, 81—Ramirez hit Florence repeatedly on her head with a hammer. He then proceeded to beat Mabel on the head. When Mabel started to scream he stripped wires from an electric clock, shocked the woman then raped her. He robbed the house but, before leaving, he took Mabel's red lipstick and drew three pentagrams, one on Mabel's thigh, one on her bedroom wall and one on Florence's. Local handyman Carlos Valenzuela noticed that the papers hadn't been picked up for two days and found the women barely alive. Florence survived but Mabel died on 17 July.

May 30, 1985

Burbank—Carol Kyle, 42 and Mark Kyle, 11—Ramirez crawled through a cat flap, woke Carol with a torch and demanded money. He threatened the boy and the woman gave him a diamond necklace. He locked Mark in a closet and proceeded to rape, sodomise and force fellation on Carol telling her: 'If you look at me again, I'll shoot you'. He then released the boy from the closet and handcuffed him to his mother before leaving. Carol Kyle provided the police with the best description they had of Ramirez, so far.

June 2, 1985

Cow Hollow, San Francisco—Theodore Wildings, 25—shot in the head while asleep. The killer then raped Nancy Brien, 25, Theodore's girlfriend. Ramirez's involvement in these crimes is disputed.

June 27, 1985

Arcadia—the Night Stalker raped a six-year-old.

June 27, 1985

Arcadia—Patty Elaine Higgins, 29—found with her throat slit.

July 2, 1985,

Arcadia—Mary Louise Cannon, 75—the grandmother of five had been beaten on the head with a vase. Ramirez then sliced her neck open with a kitchen knife before robbing the house.

July 5, 1985

Sierra Madre—Whitney Bennett, 16—struck on the head eleven times with a crow bar and almost strangled with a telephone cord before Ramirez inexplicably left her. She survived without remembering the attack and required medical treatment for the next 30 months.

July 7, 1985

Monterey Park—Joyce Lucille Nelson, 61—raped, sodomised and kicked in the head. Post mortem revealed a clear shoeprint similar to others found at other crime scenes.

July 7, 1985

Monterey Park—Linda Fortuna—Ramirez attempted to rape and sodomise Linda but could not maintain an erection. He screamed at her, but left her alive after taking her valuables.

July 20, 1985

Glendale—Maxon, 68, and Lela Kneiding, 66—both shot to death before being hacked with a machete. Forensic examination determined that the gun that killed them was the same gun that killed Veronica Yu and Dayle Okazaki. The next day the media dubbed the killer 'the Night Stalker' for the first time.

July 20, 1985

Sun Valley—Chainarong Khovananth, 32—shot to death. His wife Somkid, 29, was raped and forced to fellate the killer while lying next to her dead husband. He then sodomised the couple's eight-year-old son and left with $30 000 in cash and jewellery.

August 6, 1985

Northbridge—Christopher Peterson, 38 and his wife, Virginia 27—both survived being shot in the head. Christopher even managed to chase Ramirez away with a bullet lodged in his brain.

August 8, 1985

Diamond Bar—Elyas Abowath, 31 and wife Sakina, 27—Ramirez shot Elyas in the head then blindfolded and gagged Sakina before beating her on the head. Ramirez found the family jewels, forces Sakina to fellate him, raped and sodomised her. Three-year-old Aamar walked in and Ramirez tied a pillowcase on the boy's head before handcuffing Sakina to the doorknob and leaving. Sakina managed to free her son and persuade him to find help. The little boy found help from his neighbours.

By this time the media were broadcasting composite likenesses and descriptions of the Night Stalker. Ramirez headed north to the San Francisco area and checked into a flophouse in Tenderloin. The manager later remembered a young, gaunt, Hispanic man with rotten teeth who smelled bad. He checked out of the hotel on 17 August 1985.

August 17, 1985

Lake Merced—Peter, 66 and Barbara Pan, 64—shot in the head. Peter died that night, while Barbara survived, an invalid for the rest of her life. On the wall, in Barbara's lipstick, were an inverted pentagram and the words 'Jack the Knife'—lyrics from the song 'The Ripper' by Judas Priest. The bullets matched the LA bullets.

August 24, 1985

Mission Viejo, 50 miles (80km) south of Los Angeles—William Carns, 29—shot and wounded. Ramirez then tied up Carns' fiancée, Renata Gunter, with neckties and raped her twice. He demanded money and made her 'Swear to Satan' that she was telling the truth, which she did. He made her say 'I love Satan' before he forced her to fellate him. Then he left. Renata recovered in time to see him drive away in an orange-coloured Toyota station wagon. Police were able to trace the car because a witness had taken down the licence plate number. The police found the abandoned car and managed to lift one good fingerprint. Crosschecking revealed the identity of Richard Ramirez and his mug shot from an earlier arrest was broadcast.

Meanwhile, Ramirez attempted to steal another car from East Los Angeles. The attempt failed disastrously. Ramirez was recognised. A mob was chasing him and threatening to tear him apart before the police caught up with him. It was 31 August 1985.

Authorities charged Ramirez with 14 murders and 31 other felonies. He described himself as a 'super criminal' and said 'I love all that blood'.

The trial turned out to be one of the most complex and long criminal proceedings in the history of American law. It didn't help the case that the police quoted the defendant as saying 'Of course I did it. So what? Shoot me. I deserve to die', before launching into a humming rendition of 'Night Prowler'.

The defence began a process of delays and stalling tactics which meant that LA County Prosecutor Phil Halpin didn't even file charges until July 1988, nearly three years after Ramirez's arrest. Jury selection involved interviewing almost 1600 people. The trial finally began on 30 January 1989. The prosecution rested its case on 14 April 1989: 137 witnesses and 521 exhibits later. After hearing the case for the defence the jury started deliberations with 8000 pages of trial transcripts and 655 exhibits.

On 14 August juror Phyllis Singletary did not arrive. Her boyfriend had murdered her and committed suicide after an argument over the Ramirez case. Avoiding a mistrial, a new juror was appointed and on 20 September 1989 they reached a unanimous verdict of guilty on 13 murder counts as well as 30 other counts of burglary, sodomy and rape.

On 9 November, Richard Ramirez was sentenced to death nineteen times.

Sometimes he was coherent: 'Dying doesn't scare me ... I'll be in hell. With Satan ... big deal ... Death always went with the territory'.

Sometimes less so: 'I'll see you in Disneyland' or 'You do not understand me. I do not expect you to. You are not capable of it. I am beyond your experience. I am beyond good and evil. Legions of the night, night breed, repeat not the errors of night prowler and show no mercy. I will be avenged. Lucifer dwells within us all.'

Sometimes he was just blunt: 'You maggots make me sick'.

* * *

Freelance magazine editor, staunch Catholic and self-proclaimed virgin, Doreen Lioy, corresponded with Ramirez for years and on her third visit to him he proposed to her. She accepted and they were married on 3 October 1996.

Adam Yates, Lioy's cousin said: 'It's pretty sick. I think everybody is pretty disgusted.'

Lioy proclaims that she truly loves Ramirez and thinks he's innocent.

They have never been allowed conjugal visits.

Prisoner E37101 remains in the midst of an appeals process on Death Row at San Quentin State Prison, San Quentin, north of San Francisco California.

The Washington Snipers: John Allen Muhammad and John Lee Malvo

John Allen Williams was born on 31 December 1960 in Baton Rouge, Louisiana. *The Washington Post*, which covered the case extensively, described him as a 'serial loser'.

Completely undistinguished in high school, Williams enlisted in the American Army's National Guard in 1978.

On 22 November 1981 he married teenage sweetheart Carol Ann Kaglear and their son, Lindbergh, was born in October 1982. The marriage deteriorated to the point where Williams moved in with another woman in 1985 and enlisted in the regular army later that year.

Carol divorced him in 1987.

Although he later served in *Operation Desert Storm*, the Pentagon described his record as 'pretty unremarkable ... he barely made it' to the rank of sergeant. His former platoon leader, Rafael Miranda said: 'I don't remember him being anything special', even though he had two court-martial convictions, one for failing to report for duty and disobeying a lawful command, another for striking an officer above the left eye.

If this sort of behaviour did not make John Allen memorable one can only speculate that having two court martial convictions was common in that platoon, at that time.

Carol did all she could to keep Lindbergh away from his father.

In 1988 Williams married Mildred Green, in Tacoma Washington. They had three children. They became members of the Nation of Islam, attending a mosque in Seattle. Williams went by many names over the next 14 years and officially became Muhammad in 2001.

He ran a car-repair business, which failed and started a karate school, which also failed.

After years of putting up with Muhammad's frequently erratic, gun-happy behaviour—'he could make a weapon out of anything,' she said—and his endless mind games Mildred filed for divorce in 1999.

In late March 2000, Muhammad kidnapped his children from school and took them to St Johns, Antigua. Mildred was hospitalised in Tacoma and Muhammad took the opportunity to call her and threaten to kill her.

While in St Johns, Muhammad made a sporadic living repairing cars, but was also involved in a variety of scams to make a quick buck here and there, including a sideline in document forging. Although he wasn't very good at this either, he was good enough to acquire Antiguan citizenship, using false papers.

In August 2000, Una James and her son, John Lee Malvo, moved into a house in St Johns. On 1 November, James said she would be returning to Jamaica to visit her sick mother. Two weeks later she still had not come back.

At some point during this time, Muhammad decided to 'adopt' Malvo and the lonely, neglected and somewhat abused boy, then 15, moved in with Muhammad and his three children.

In May 2001 Muhammad told the people he knew that he was moving the family to Canada. When he left Antigua he took Malvo with him—illegally.

Returning instead to America, Muhammad enrolled his children under false names in Bellingham, 100 miles north of Tacoma. On 31 October 2001 police traced them and returned them to their mother. Mildred Muhammad had had enough and quietly went underground, disappearing to Clinton in Prince George's County, Maryland. She never saw her husband again, but later she said that she believed that he knew where she was and that he intended to kill her, eventually.

Muhammad looked for her for three months, then, failing to find her, vanished. Having lost custody of his own children and unable to trace his wife, Muhammad was left with his 'adopted' son John Lee Malvo.

In October 2001 Muhammad and Malvo were living together as father and son at the Lighthouse Mission, a homeless shelter in Bellingham.

Drifting and supporting himself and Malvo anyway he could, Muhammad began to weave the young man into his bizarre world. Muhammad and Malvo went in and out of many people's lives over the coming months, telling any number of stories and suckering any number of well-intentioned people, exploiting the kindness of strangers. It helped that Muhammad had 30 cousins and he made use of some of these connections too.

In between trips and visits, fuelled by Muhammad's ongoing resentment at having lost two families, Muhammad and Malvo became a two-man execution squad.

The killings were almost totally random:

February 16, 2002

7 pm—Tacoma, Washington—Muhammad is on the hunt for Isa Nichols, a former bookkeeper for his defunct car-repair business, who had testified against him at the custody hearing with Mildred, but that night, Isa is out shopping with her daughter. Instead, while her six-month-old daughter, Angelaeh is waiting for her bath, Isa's niece Keenya Cook, 21, answers her aunt's front door bell. She is shot with a .45 calibre pistol. The bullet enters her face below her left eye and lodges at the base

of her skull. The house is filling with smoke from food burning on the stove when her aunt and cousin return and find her body. The baby is asleep upstairs. It is two days before John Lee Malvo's 17th birthday.

March 19, 2002

midday—Tucson, Arizona—keen golfer and frozen foods salesman, Jerry Ray Taylor, 60, is chipping balls alone in a practice area at Fred Enke golf course when a high-powered rifle shoots him in the back. The bullet tears through his heart and kills him instantly. The killers drag the body into nearby scrub. Two golfers find Taylor's body that afternoon. Nearby is his wallet—cash and credit cards still inside. Several weeks later, while visiting his friend Harjeet Singh in Bellingham, Muhammad boasts that while on a trip to Arizona, he killed 'a pair of elderly golfers.' Singh doesn't believe him. Police later establish that no other golfer was shot in the State at that time.

July 2, 2000

a firearms distributor delivers a Bushmaster XM-15—the civilian version of the military's M-16 rifle—to the Bull's Eye Shooter Supply gun shop in Tacoma. The US$1600 weapon has a bi-pod, telescopic sight and a targeting laser. It disappears from the store, but the owner does not realise it's missing until months later—after Muhammad and Malvo are arrested. Muhammad now visits an old Army buddy in Tacoma, Robert Holmes, and shows him his new toy. Holmes observes that his strange friend is becoming even stranger: 'The outer shell looked the same, but there were some little quirks in the armour ... Some of the things he was saying—I knew there was something wrong.'

September 5, 2002

10:30 pm—Clinton, Prince George's County, Maryland—eerily close to the house of Sheron Norman, Mildred Muhammad's sister. Outside Margellina's Pizzeria the owner, Paul LaRuffa, 55, is behind the wheel of his car and about to leave. The gunmen attack him with a .22 calibre pistol. Half a dozen bullets tear into his chest, back and left arm. The gunman grabs LaRuffa's laptop and the day's takings of $3500. As he bleeds, LaRuffa promises himself: 'I'm not going to die in a parking lot in Clinton, Maryland' and he survives.

On 10 September 2002—Muhammad bought a blue Chevrolet Caprice for $250 from the ironically named Sure Shot Auto Sales in Trenton, New Jersey. Before buying the car he asked if it has a jack and a spare tire because he plans to drive to Washington.

September 14, 2002

10 pm—Hillandale, Montgomery County, Alabama—Arnie Zelkowivitz is shot while showing an employee how to shut his liquor store. He survives.

September 15, 2000

10 pm—Brandywine, Montgomery County, Alabama—two bullets fired past the head of Muhammad Rashid, 32, as he closes the Three Road Liquor Store. A third bullet strikes him in the abdomen. Rashid survives by playing dead as the gunmen steal his wallet.

September 21, 2002

12:15 am—in the car park of Sammy's Package Store in Atlanta, Georgia. One .22 calibre pistol bullet hits Million A. Woldermariam, 41, in the back of the head and another in his back as he leaves work. He dies not long after.

September 21, 2002

7 pm—Montgomery, Alabama—two shots hit Claudine Parker, 52, and Kellie Adams, 24, as they close a state-run ABC Liquor Store. A passing policeman sees a man holding a pistol and standing over the victims. The man runs off and police later find the nickel-plated, .22 calibre revolver along the shooter's escape route. Claudine Parker dies later. Kellie Adams, though shot in the base of the head, survives and later becomes a vital witness for the prosecution.

The police were now on full alert. They set up a help line and received a call from someone they believed to be the sniper. The caller claims to have committed a robbery and slaying in the South. This call and a fingerprint left at the scene leads police to the Alabama shooting, then to the Tacoma shooting, prompting them to look for a 1990 blue Chevrolet with New Jersey licence plate NDA 21Z, owned by John Muhammad.

September 23, 2002

6:30 pm—Baton Rouge, Louisiana—Hong Im Ballenger, 45, is walking to her 4WD after finishing work at the Beauty Depot when a bullet from the Bushmaster strikes her in the head, fatally.

From then on, Muhammad and Malvo become the true Washington Snipers. For three weeks the people of Maryland, Virginia and Washington, DC are kept in an almost constant state of fear. It seems that the riskiest thing that you can do is simply mind your own business—and visit a petrol station.

October 2, 2002

Montgomery County, Maryland.
5:20 pm—Michaels Craft Store, 13850 Georgia Ave, Aspen Hill—store window shot. No injuries.
6:04 pm—Shoppers Food Warehouse, 2201 Randolph Rd, Wheaton—James D Martin, 55, shot and killed while crossing the car park.

October 3, 2002

Montgomery County, Maryland.
7:41 am Fitzgerald Auto Mall, 11411 Rockville Pike, White Flint. James L 'Sonny' Buchanan, 39, shot and killed while mowing his lawn.
8:12 am—Mobil petrol station, Aspen Hill Rd and Connecticut Ave, Aspen Hill—Premkumar A. Walekar, 54 shot and killed while at the petrol pump.
8:37 am—post office near Leisure World, 3701 Rossmoor Blvd, Silver Spring—Sarah Ramos, 34, shot in the head and killed while sitting on a park bench.
9:58 am—Shell petrol station, Knowles and Connecticut Avenues, Kensington—Lori Ann Lewis-Rivera, 25, shot and killed while vacuuming her minivan.

October 3, 2003

Washington, DC.
9:20 pm—street corner, Georgia Ave and Kalmia Rd North Washington—Pascal Charlot, 72, shot below the neck and killed while crossing the street.

October 4, 2003

Spotsylvania County, Virginia.
2:30 p.m—at the car park of Michael's Craft Store, Spotsylvania County, 1390 feet (424 metres) from the entrance to the Interstate-95, a 43-year-old woman is shot in the back while loading packages into her car but is admitted to hospital in a stable condition.

October 7, 2003

Prince George's County, Maryland.
8:08 am—at Benjamin Tasker Middle School, 4901 Collington Rd, Bowie—880 feet from the nearest entrance to Route 50, a 13-year-old student is shot in the chest after he is dropped off for school. Admitted to hospital in a critical condition, he survived.

During the shootings, schools throughout the area refused to allow outdoor recess. Some parents kept their children at home, terrified to let them out. Athletic events and outdoor activities throughout the region were cancelled and shops reported declining sales as people refused to leave their homes.

October 9, 2003

Manassas, Prince William County, Virginia.
8:18 pm—at Sunoco petrol station at 7203 Sudley Rd, Prince William County, 940 feet (287 metres) from the nearest entrance to Interstate-66—Dean Harold Meyers, 53, had just bought petrol and was about to climb back into his car when he was shot in the head and killed.

October 11, 2003

Fredericksburg, Spotsylvania County, Virginia.
9:30 am—at the Exxon petrol station, Route 1 and Market St, Spotsylvania County—Kenneth Bridges, 53, shot and killed while pumping petrol.

October 14, 2003

Fairfax County, Virginia.
9:15 pm—in the car park on the lower level of the Seven Corners Shopping Centre in Fairfax County—Linda Franklin, 47, is shot and killed while loading packages into her car.

October 19, 2003

Ashland, Virginia.
7:59 pm—at the parking lot of the Ponderosa Steakhouse, 809 England St, Ashland, Virginia—a shot comes from a wooded area, about 300 yards (275m) west of an Interstate-95 entrance ramp. A 37-year-old man is shot and wounded while walking to his car with his wife after dinner.

October 22, 2003

Montgomery County, Maryland.
5:59 a.m—at the intersection of Grand Pre Rd and Connecticut Ave in Aspen Hill, Maryland—Conrad Johnson, 35, is shot in his upper stomach and dies soon after.

As if these killings and woundings weren't terrible enough, on 23 October 2002, Mark Cosslett, a 16-year-veteran of the Virginia State Police, visited his two-year-old son's school to reassure his classmates and teachers that the police were doing their best. In a region gripped by fear Cosslett felt duty-bound to work even on his day off. When he received a call that witnesses had heard shots on the Interstate-95 near Springfield Cosslett, he immediately went to investigate. A tow-truck veered into his path and he died of his injuries in hospital at 5:30 pm that afternoon.

Tragically, the shots had nothing to do with the Washington Snipers.

At approximately 1 am on Thursday, 24 October 2002 a motorist called the emergency hotline to report seeing a 1990 Chevy Caprice, bearing New Jersey licence plate NDA 21Z, parked in the rest stop at the corner of Interstate-70 and mile marker 42, 11 miles (17.7 km) west of Frederick City Maryland. A police taskforce investigated and found John Allen Muhammad and Lee Malvo asleep in the car. They were apprehended without much incident.

Police found Paul LaRuffa's laptop in the car and determined almost immediately that the vehicle had been modified so someone could lie in the back of the car and shoot. Ballistics experts established that the Bushmaster rifle found in the car was the murder weapon in eight of the 10 deaths. Evidence for the shootings of James D Martin and James L Buchanan was inconclusive at the time, but was later established in court. Muhammad and Malvo were separated and would remain separated. Prince William County would eventually oversee Muhammad, while Fairfax County dealt with Malvo.

***

An article published in the *Gazette.Net* on 17 October 2002 partially redressed the oft-cited criticism that, as a society, we tend to glamorise killers and forget the victims.

Feel free to look up the article at:
http://gazette.net/gazette_archive/2002/200242/montgomeryctv/county/126097-1.html

***

When his capital murder trial began in 2003 Muhammad could not afford an attorney and, although two were assigned to his case, he chose to represent himself. As usual, he proved that those who choose to represent themselves in court usually have incompetents for counsel and idiots for clients. As Muhammad interrogated witnesses his aggressive style alienated the jury and, as the prosecution pursued its case, the Sniper realised that he was in way over his head and his legal counsel was soon in charge again. In the face of the mountain of evidence against both of them it was all pretty pointless. On Monday, 17 November 2003, after 6½ hours of deliberation, the jury found Muhammad guilty of the killing of Dean H Meyers and guilty of killing at least one other person in the previous three years—enough for a capital conviction.

Willie Jean Nichols, grandmother of Keenya Cook, said the time: 'Closure is not something I understand. There won't be any closure for us, due to the fact Keenya is not coming back.'

***

On account of his age at the time of the shootings, Malvo was sentenced to a life term in prison without parole.

On 22 April 2005, the Virginia Supreme Court upheld Muhammad's convictions and death sentence, including a capital conspiracy charge based on a new antiterrorism law, which came into effect as a result of the September 2001 attack on the World Trade Centre in New York.

Before dawn on Monday, 24 August 2005 Muhammad was driven from Death Row in Sussex County, Virginia, prison and ultimately ended up at the Clarksburg correctional facility in Maryland. Both Muhammad and Malvo have been indicted to stand trial for the Montgomery County shootings. Malvo had already been transferred in May 2005 but Muhammad fought the extradition as long as he could.

On 2 September 2005, a Maryland judge set trial dates for the snipers: Muhammad for 1 May 2006 and John Lee Malvo on 10 October 2006 for the six counts of first-degree murder in Maryland.

***

The Washington Snipers' trials are estimated to have so far cost at least US$3 million. John Lee Muhammad will continue to cost the American taxpayer a lot of money. In an article in the Washington Post, dated 23 August 2005, Montgomery Sheriff Raymond M Kight estimated that securing the courthouse alone could cost $400 000.

Louisiana and Alabama also have plans to prosecute Muhammad and Malvo on murder charges.

Milestones on the Last Mile

2 December 2005: Van Tuong Nguyen

Not all people who die for their crimes are murderers. The story of Van Nguyen is very different from the Ted Bundys, John Wayne Gacys and Night Stalkers of the world. He was the first Australian arrested and subsequently executed for drug trafficking in Singapore. Extraordinary as this is, the facts of Van's life are in many ways typical of people who are on Death Row outside America and whose circumstances are a more accurate reflection of crimes that may not be born so much from malice as from desperation.

On August 17 1980 Van Tuong Nguyen and his twin brother Khoa were born in a refugee camp in Sonkha, Thailand. His own words speak more eloquently of his life than any newspaper report. The following quotes are from his trial transcripts, recorded between 2002 and 2004.

> 'My mother was a Vietnamese refugee. I did not know who my father was until November this year. He came from America to look for my brother and I. I had a twin brother and no other sibling. Shortly after I was born, I followed my mother together with my twin brother and migrated to Australia. I cannot remember much about my childhood. My mother married in 1987 to a

> Vietnamese Australian. My stepfather beat my brother and I quite often. I went to St Joseph Primary School in Springvale, Melbourne when I was about six years old. When I was 12 years old, I went to the Mt Waverley Secondary College. I completed secondary school education in 1998 when I was about 18 years old. Then I intended to proceed with my university education at Deakin University. However due to financial difficulties, I started working instead of studying. I worked as storeman, door-to-door salesman, computer sales and research marketing. Around end 1999, I also set up my own business in Melbourne dealing with computer sales. There was no need for any capital. Shortly after that my twin brother got into trouble with the law and I wind up my business to raise legal fees for him. So I found a sale, research and marketing job and I earned between A$1500 to A$2500 a month depending on how much commission I received. I took long leave since June this year (2003) as I was on medication for acne that required four months' leave.'

The event that first drew the world's attention to Van occurred after he fell asleep at Changi Airport, Singapore on 12 December 2002. When he woke up he rushed to catch his plane, but neglected to put his mobile phone through the security scanner. The phone set of the metal detector and the authorities instigated a standard search. That's when they discovered the heroin: all 396.2 grams of it.

This is what the trial transcript had to say:

> 'He is an Australian national aged 23 years. On 12 December 2002 he arrived in Singapore from Phnom Penh (Cambodia). At about 7.45 pm he was at Boarding Gate C22 of the airport waiting to board a flight to Melbourne. During a routine check, a police officer felt something bulky on his lower back. He was brought to a search room for a thorough search, taking his haversack and business bag with him.
>
> In the search room he was asked to remove his jacket and shirt. When that was done, a plastic packet was seen strapped to

his lower back with masking tape. At that stage he started crying and tried to hit his head against a wall.

Sergeant Teh Kim Leng ('Sgt Teh'), the officer in charge of the security screening unit, was notified. He went to the search room and saw the accused, who appeared to be in distress, holding his head with his hands. When Sgt Teh asked him what was on his back, the accused replied that it was heroin. With the help of Sgt Teh the accused removed the packet from his body. When Sgt Teh asked him if there was anything to declare in his luggage, the accused opened the haversack, took out another packet, and handed it to him.

The two packets were subsequently sent for analysis. The packet from the body was found to contain not less than 151.5g of diamorphine and the other packet not less than 244.7g. The analysis results were not disputed.'

***

The initial interview at the airport reads like a page from a suspense novel:

Q: 'What [is] this?'
A: 'I know it [is] heroin although different colour.'
Q: 'Number 3 or 4?'
A: 'I don't know.'
Q: 'Who asked you to bring?'
A: 'I know him by Sun.'
Q: 'To bring where?'
A: 'Melbourne and someone [will] take from me or maybe Sydney.'
Q: 'Who will receive the drug at Australia?'
A: 'Someone will recognised [sic] me and [tell] me he likes basketball.'

★★★

The next day at 4:05 pm authorities spent two hours taking a 'cautioned statement'. His words provide a detailed account of how, exactly, someone comes to be in the position he was in.

★★★

> 'I am known as "Van" to my friends and family members.
>
> Sometime in October this year, I was in need of money. I had to paya debt, which I took to pay for my twin brother, Khoa Nguyen, lawyer fees. I owed about A$20 000 to A$25 000 in total to a friend. My friend is Jonathan Lim, Australia Chinese. He did not press me for payment but I knew he needed the money. There was also an A$12 000 loan which my twin brother took that I needed to repay on his behalf. He only had until the end of this year to pay up that loan. I did not intend to let my twin brother know that I am paying his debt. I had managed only to repay about A$4000 for a period of eight to 10 months already but that was just enough to cover for the interests incurred. The A$4000 was my earnings from my job as a sales marketing executive. My brother's lawyer's fees were as a result of one drug case and one affray case he got into about 3 years ago. Since then my brother had been in debts. I had been helping him in the repayment of loans for the entire three years.'

★★★

The situation became progressively worse for Van Nguyen. By October 2002 he had been out of work for four months and owed rent money. Then:

> 'Sometime in the first week of November, a male Chinese known to me as "Tan" contacted me. He asked me whether I was sure I would do something. I told him yes. Then he told me to go to Sydney in one week's time. He did not tell me what was the purpose for the trip. He just instructed me to go to a hotel called Pacific International when I arrived at Sydney and

someone would contact me there. I had earlier asked him for help and told him that I needed quick money. His response to me at that time was he would see what he could do.

Sometime in mid November this year, I made a trip to Sydney following "Tan's" instructions. When I arrived at Pacific International Hotel, one male Vietnamese "Sun" contacted me. He explained to me exactly what I am going to do and asked me if I am going to do it. He told me that I would be carrying a package from Cambodia to Singapore to Melbourne and possibly Sydney. He told me that the package contained "white". I understood that as heroin. It could have been cocaine. But I do not know if it is heroin or cocaine. However I was quite certain that it contained drugs. I told 'Sun' that I would do it. "Sun" then told me to return to the same hotel to look for him before 2 Dec 2002 for the job. "Sun" told me that the deal was confirmed and I would definitely be making the trip to carrying that package. After that I returned to Melbourne.

On the 1 Dec 2002, I made the second trip for Sydney to go to hotel Pacific International where I met up with "Sun". He handed to me a return airfare from Melbourne to Singapore to Phnom Penh. He instructed me to go to Pacific Hotel when I reached Phnom Penh and to go to a restaurant across the road called "Lucky Burger" on the 4th and 5th of Dec 02. Someone was supposed to meet me there.

On the 4th Dec 2002, I went to the "Lucky Burger" restaurant at 3 pm as directed by "Sun" to wait for someone. I waited for about half an hour there and a male Cambodian approached me. He told me to follow him and I did so. He led me to his car and took me somewhere. A man who could speak Vietnamese showed up. He told me to smoke heroin. I refused. He yelled at me but I did not understand what he was shouting about. He then threatened me by saying, "smoke! Or else …" I was under fear and so I had to smoke heroin.'

***

Further facts emerged on 15 December 2002. The 'somewhere' of the previous statement turned out to be a garage shed.

> 'There were altogether three people there including the man who brought me there. I had never seen them before. The man who spoke Vietnamese did not tell me his name nor did he identify himself in any way. They already had the equipment for consuming heroin prepared on a table. There were an aluminium foil and a rolled-up Cambodian note. The man who brought me there took out from his pocket a plastic containing heroin and a lighter and placed them on the table. He then offered the heroin to me to consume. I hesitated and refused. I got aggressive and told him no. That was when the man who spoke Vietnamese stood up and told me in partial Vietnamese and partial Cambodian language, 'f— your mother, smoke or die'. That was when I realised he had a rod in his hand as he hit it hard on a bench. I then knew that I could be killed if I do not follow what they told me to do.'

On December 5, 2002 at about 3pm Van Nguyen was back in the garage:

> 'The Vietnamese speaking man told me to take off my shirt. I asked him why and he told me just take it off. I then took off my shirt. He then took out 2 blocks of substance wrapped in tapes. I did not know what they contained at that point in time. He then took the 2 blocks and placed them on my back. I asked him why he was doing that. He told me that someone would come to see me and prepare everything for me in that manner on the 10 Dec 02. He also told me that that was how the 2 blocks would be positioned and this is the way I was going to bring the package back to Melbourne. I was told to be at 'Lucky Burger' at 4 pm on the 10 Dec 02.'

***

As it turned out, he didn't make that appointment, but:

***

'The next day, on the 11 Dec 2002 at about 3 pm, I went to 'Lucky Burger' restaurant. I went there hoping that they would be there. At about 4 pm, the same person who came to pick me up during the first 2 occasions appeared. Again, he asked me to follow him in his car. We arrived at the same garage.

At the garage, the man who spoke Vietnamese started scolding me. He asked me if I was a cop or a policeman. I was then stripped and searched. Again, they asked me to smoke heroin. I explained to them it was not a good idea to consume drug before travelling from countries to countries. They accepted that and did not force me any further. They then passed a bag containing a sealer, rolls of plastic, scissors, gloves, Velcro tapes, super glue, handy-knives and some other accessories. There was also an electric coffee blender.

The Vietnamese speaking man then instructed me to crush the 2 rocks of heroin using the coffee blender into fine powdery form. As he explained, the man who brought me there brought out 2 rocks of heroin. They are rectangular in shape and white in colour. Each rock was contained inside a plastic bag. The Vietnamese speaking man told me that the person who was supposed to help me strapped the package was gone somewhere else. I told him that he was supposed to solve that problem. That was when I was threatened not to mess things up. No more things were said. He then told me that I would have to strap the package on my own. He told me first to crush both the rock of heroin separately using the coffee blender. He also reminded me not to mix the two rocks of heroin at any time. Then I was to seal them inside two plastic bags using those things they gave me inside the bag. He then told me to strap the two plastic packets of powdered heroin onto my back. He then handed over the bag and warned me not to back out or chicken out again. I asked him if he were sure that the two plastic packets of heroin to be strapped to my back and he again warned me not to mess it up as someone would be watching over me.

After collecting the two rocks of heroin and the bag containing all the tools, I was sent back to my hotel room. When I reached my room, I went left everything inside my room and went to a shop nearby to buy a hammer and a power adapter. The hammer is for breaking the heroin rock into smaller bits so that they could be fitted into the coffee blender. The power adapter is to connect the sealer to a powerpoint. Then I returned to my hotel room and started preparing the crushing of the rock heroin.'

***

Although there was a final statement on 19 December most of the full story emerged with the third statement on 16 December 2003. By his own account, Van Nguyen wasn't cut out to be a heroin smuggler.

***

'At my hotel room, I took out everything from the bag. I planned in what process I would do to package the two rocks of heroin. I decided that some of the equipment could be used while some could not be used and I separate them apart. I took out one rock of heroin and placed it into a plastic bag and started to break it into smaller pieces using the hammer. It took about an hour or so. After that I placed all the smaller bits into the coffee blender portion by portion. That took about an hour also. Then I poured all the powderise heroin onto a plastic and sealed the plastic using the sealer. I repeated the same process for the second rock of heroin. At the end of that, I had two sealed plastic containing powderise heroin. I tried to packed the two plastic as slim as possible. But I did not really know how to go about doing that, so I just did what I thought would work. I also realised there were still some small rocks still not powderise. I did not bother to re-do as I was tired to repeat the process again.

I then rested and thought of how to strap the two plastic package onto my back. I realised that I needed sticky tapes to do it. There was no sticky tapes found inside the bag which the Vietnamese speaking man gave me. There was only a Velcro tape that I was not sure how they wanted me to do it. At about 10 am on the 12 Dec 02, I went to purchase sticky tapes from a shop around the corner near the hotel.

Then I returned to my hotel room and started to strap the two plastic packets onto my back. However, I could only managed to strap one plastic packet around my lower back using the yellow tapes that I just bought. The second plastic packet I was unable to reach my upper back on my own. I decided to strap it around my abdomen. I then used the remaining yellow tapes and the white colour tapes to secure the two plastic packets around my lower back and my abdomen as tight as I could. I then wore my under-garment and also put on my clothing.

On the same day, 12 Dec 2002, at about 11 am I carried my luggage and went downstairs and checked out of the hotel. I reached the airport at about 11.45 am At the airport twice the security officers there checked me. However they did not discover the two packets of heroin strapped on my body. I boarded Silkair flight, MI 622, heading for Singapore at 12.20 pm

During my flight, I started to have difficulties in breathing. I then went to the toilet and removed the package that was strapped to my abdomen. I then placed it into my pants and tugged out my shirt so that it was not obvious to be seen.

I went back to my seat and secretly stuffed the package that I took off in the toilet into my backpack.

On the same day at about 3.20 pm I arrived at Changi International Airport Terminal 2 in Singapore. I went to the duty free shop at Terminal 2 and bought a carton of Marlboro Menthol Lights cigarettes. I then went to the smoking room and smoked a cigarette. Then I went took the skytrain to Terminal 1 as I was instructed by the information counter that my flight back to Melbourne was at Terminal 1.

I then went to the shower room to have a look at my packages. I removed the tapes that were still stuck on the plastic packet that was hidden inside my backpack. I threw the tapes into a rubbish bin inside the shower room. I then place this plastic packet of heroin into the back compartment of the backpack. I did not do anything to the plastic packet of heroin that was strapped to my lower back.

After that I went back to the lounge and slept. I woke up at about 7.30 pm and my flight was at 7.40 pm My flight number was QF 10. I thought that I was late and so I run to gate C22 from the lounge. I took about 5 minutes to run to Gate C22.

At the gate C22, I took a good glance to see if anyone was watching. I was looking for the drug syndicate people to see if anyone was really watching over me. However I was not able to tell if I was being watched. So I decided that it was too late to turn back. I was also worried about the safety of my family members as the people in Phnom Penh warned me that the syndicate knew where I lived and warned me not to messed up. I knew that they were implying should I messed it up, they will be looking for me at my house or my family members in Melbourne. I had no choice but to deliver the two packets of heroin to someone in Australia.

At the metal detector, I placed my backpack and my business bag onto the X-ray machine. Then I walked through the metal detector and as I was crossing, it beeped. At that point in time, I knew I was going to be caught. A policewoman told me stand one side so as not to obstruct traffic. She then used a metal detector wand to search me by going up and down my body. The metal detector wand did not beep. She then touched my back, either using her hand or the metal detector wand, and when she reached my lower back, she must have discovered the packet of heroin strapped there. She asked me, "what is this?" I shook my head and said, 'No'. She then asked a male colleague to bring me to a room to search me. I requested to bring the backpack and business bag to the room as well, which she allowed.

Inside the room, the male officer asked me to put my hands on the wall. I told him, "no need, I will get it for you." I lifted up my shirt and pulled out the strapped packet on my lower back and gave it to the officer. He asked me what that was and I replied to him, "It's heroin, sir". He asked me if I was sure. I told him of course. I also told him that there was more and I went on to retrieve the packet of heroin which I had hidden inside my backpack.'

***

In a country that has a mandatory death penalty for those carrying as little as 15 grams it would seem from that moment that Van was doomed, yet there are some who argue that he wasn't.

Craig Skehan and Connie Levett quote Singaporean lawyer Subhas Anandan—in their article in the *Sydney Morning Herald* of 3 December 2005—as saying that the Australian government should have made representation to Singapore early on to attempt to have the charges lowered to a non-capital offence. In the end it may have been Van's basic decent nature that doomed him. The young, first offender cooperated with Singapore police, providing a full confession, virtually handing Singapore authorities a complete case against him. In a climate of mandatory sentencing, Van's mitigating circumstances were worthless—Singapore judges simply had no discretion in the matter.

By the time Van's trial began on 24 November 2003 his ultimate execution was virtually a foregone conclusion. Only the Singapore government could have saved him, and it wasn't about to compromise what it saw as its sovereignty to do so.

On 20 March 2004 the Singapore High Court sentenced Van to death under the *Misuse of Drugs Act*. The High Court dismissed an application for clemency on 20 October 2004. The Singaporean government then rejected a direct appeal from the Australian government on 21 October 2005.

On 3 November Singapore's Minister for Foreign Affairs, George Yeo, further affirmed Singapore's commitment to apply the death penalty. On 17 November, Australian Prime Minister John Howard made an unsuccessful appeal to Singapore's Prime Minister, Lee Hsien Hong, on the same day that Van's family received a letter informing them that he was scheduled to be hanged on 2 December.

In spite of increasingly loud voices from Australia and throughout the world condemning the execution including candlelight vigils and rallies, from the Singaporean point of view the West's protest not only counted as meddling in internal affairs but it also smacked of hypocrisy. Culturally it's probably hard to forget that the British Empire had quite happily exploited millions of people in the opium trade. If the Singaporeans and other Asian nations have taken a hard line against drugs perhaps it's because they haven't forgotten how many lives drug users and traffickers have ruined. It would seem that Asian cultures have longer memories than Western ones.

If many Australians regard his death as cruel and unnecessary and the Singaporeans as barbarians they should know that on 30 November 2005, 47 per cent of those Australians that Roy Morgan Research interviewed in fact agreed that Van Nguyen should hang.

***

And hang he did: at 6:00 am Singapore time on 2 December 2005. All the media attention, the candlelight vigils and protests were never going to change that. His mother, Kim, wasn't even allowed to give him a hug goodbye. Van's body was flown to Australia on Sunday 4 December 2005 and was later buried in Melbourne.

Kenneth Lee Boyd

By one of those bizarre coincidences that emerge in history from time to time another milestone execution took place on 2 December 2005.

Kenneth Lee Boyd was born on 19 January 1948. He left school in the ninth grade, joined the army in 1966 and volunteered to serve in Vietnam in 1967. He received an honourable discharge in 1969. His first marriage produced a son, Kenneth Smith, born in 1970. After that marriage ended in divorce, Boyd married Julie Curry in 1974. By all accounts the marriage was unhappy and constantly punctuated by separations and temporary reconciliations. Julie left him in early 1988 taking their three sons to live with Julie's father, Thomas Dillard Curry. Boyd stalked Julie, reportedly once handing one of their sons a bullet with a note to Julie telling her that the bullet was for her.

On 4 March 1988 he went to his father-in-law's house, a .357 Magnum pistol in his hand. As he said later:

> 'I walked to the back door and opened it. It was unlocked. As I walked in, I saw a silhouette that I believe was Dillard. It was just like I was in Vietnam. I pulled the gun out and started shooting. I think I shot Dillard one time and he fell. Then I walked past

> him and into the kitchen and living room area. The whole time I was pointing and shooting. Then I saw another silhouette that I believe was Julie come out of the bedroom. I shot again, probably several times. Then I reloaded my gun. I dropped the empty shell casings onto the floor. As I reloaded, I heard someone groan, Julie I guess. I turned and aimed, shooting again.'

As Julie fell she collapsed onto her son Christopher, pinning him under her. Boyd continued to fire as Julie moaned and Christopher struggled to escape by clambering under a bed. Another son tried to take the gun from his father while Boyd tried to reload. Boyd finally stopped shooting and called 911. He told the emergency operator: 'I've shot my wife and her father. Come on and get me.' At this point he thought about escaping.

> 'My only thoughts were to shoot my way out of the house. I kept pointing and shooting at anything that moved. I went back out the same door that I came in and I saw a big guy pointing a gun at me. I think this was Craig Curry, Julie's brother. I shot at him three or four times as I was running towards the woods.'

The Boyd's boys were only 13, 12 and 10 when they watched their father kill their mother and grandfather before their very eyes.

Boyd was indicted on 16 May 1988. Dr Patricio Lara and Dr John Warren testified that Boyd suffered from adjustment disorder, obsessive-compulsive disorder, dependant personality disorder and chronic depression all aggravated by alcohol abuse. On 14 July 1994, the Rockingham County Superior Court sentenced him to death for the two murders. He spent eleven years on Death Row.

On the day of his execution Kenneth Smith—who had not witnessed the events of 4 March 1988—visited his father. His wife and their two children accompanied him. Boyd's final words were to his daughter-in-law, who witnessed the actual execution. He asked that she look after his son and his grandchildren. He also asked that 'God help everybody in here.'

After his last meal of New York strip steak, a baked potato with sour cream, salad with ranch dressing and cola, Boyd died by lethal injection at 2:15 am on 2 December 2005 at the Central Prison in Raleigh, North Carolina.

He was the 1000th prisoner executed in America since the resumption of the death penalty in 1977.

Two days before his death he said: 'I'd hate to be remembered as that. I don't like the idea of being picked as a number.'

★★★

Later that same night South Carolina executed prisoner 1001, Shawn Humphries, for the 1994 murder of Max-Saver convenience store owner Mendal Alton 'Dickie' Smith. As he was about to die Humphries spoke to Dickie's sisters. 'I'm sorry,' he said through the viewing window of the execution chamber.

December 13 2005: Stanley Tookie Williams

One of the more interesting debates about this whole capital punishment thing strikes at the heart of the idea of punishment itself. Just who are you punishing and what are you punishing them for? One elegant argument goes like this: the person you are yesterday is not the person you are today. It stands to reason then that the person who committed a crime may not be the person who you punish for the crime. If jail is supposed to be corrective, then what do you do if the correction works? What happens if, for whatever reason, a jail actually accomplishes its job and makes a new person out of someone? How do you deal with that? That's what makes the Tookie Williams case so controversial. Did the State of California, did Governor Schwarznegger kill someone who not only would never kill again (assuming he did in the first place) but who was also doing a lot of good? Or at least trying to?

When Stanley Tookie Williams III was born 29 December 1953, in New Orleans, Louisiana, his mother was only 17 years old. They moved to poor and crime-ridden South Central Los Angeles in 1956. Tookie grew up to be a street fighter. In 1969 Raymond 'Truck' Washington formed a street gang on South Central East Side called the Crips—a corruption of the word 'cribs' that was a reference to the youthfulness of the gang. In 1971 Tookie and Washington formed the West Side Crips as a sort of grass roots vigilante movement to clean up the streets, but things went sour early on and the Crips turned into yet one more part of the problem, rather than the solution.

According to an accomplice known only in court records as 'Daryl', on 27 February 1979, Williams used a sawn-off shotgun to kill 23-year-old Albert Lewis Owens, the father of two daughters. Tookie shot the clerk of the 7-Eleven Store at 10437 Whittier Boulevard to eliminate any witnesses of a holdup that netted the princely sum of $120 to the four robbers: Tookie, Daryl, Alfred 'Blackie' Coward and Tony Sims. Coward later testified that Tookie said he killed Owens 'because he was white [and he was] killing all white people.'

'You should have heard the way he sounded when I shot him,' Tookie allegedly said as he made fun of the noises that Owens made as he died.

Tsai-Shen Yang, 63, and her husband Yen-Yi Yang, 73, emigrated from Taiwan in 1973. In July 1975 they purchased the Brookhaven Motel at 10411 South Vermont Avenue in South Central Los Angeles, which they ran with their son Robert. Their daughter Ye-Chen Lin, 43, mother of two sons, 14 and 13 and one daughter, 10, was visiting from Taiwan when, at around 5:00 am on 11 March 1979, the sound of someone breaking down the door to the motel's office woke Robert. He heard a woman's scream, then gunshots. By the time he reached the office he found the bodies of his parents and sister and an empty cash register. All had been shot at close range for the slightly less princely sum of $100.

Although there were no witnesses Tookie was taken into custody and tried on the evidence of his peers, cohorts, cronies and accomplices, among them his housemate James Garrett. He was arrested on 15 March 1979, convicted and sentenced to death in a Torrance, California courtroom on four counts of first-degree murder on 5 April 1981.

From the very beginning Tookie maintained his innocence, alleging false testimony, misconduct by the prosecution, incompetent defence and deals that ensured the immunity of those testifying against him. This stance led to a round of appeals that lasted over two decades.

In the beginning he was hardly a model prisoner. He spent 6½ years in solitary confinement during the 1980s for assaulting fellow prisoners and prison guards alike. A particular low point was 10 October 1988 when fellow Death Row inmate and Crips member, Tiequon Aundray Cox, stabbed him in retaliation for another stabbing Tookie allegedly 'ordered.'

In the 1990s Tookie began acting like another person entirely, more like Stanely Williams than Tookie Williams. He wrote books about life in prison, including *Blue Rage, Black Redemption*. He made public service announcements against gang violence and began writing a series of books aimed at warning kids about gangs and street life. Swiss Parliament member, Mario Fehr, nominated him for the Nobel Peace Prize every year from 2001 to 2005. Politicians, celebrities and many members of the public throughout the world became involved in launching clemency petitions, as Stanley's change of heart and active work to discourage kids from joining gangs became better known.

Twenty-four years after the Los Angeles murders the cable channel *FX* screened a movie based on Stanley's life: *Redemption*. Lora Owens, the stepmother who had raised Albert Owens, was not impressed. 'I'm outraged they'd even call it *Redemption* ... He shot him not once, but twice in the back. He didn't do anything to deserve it. He begged for his life. I believe Williams needs to get the punishment he was given when he was tried and sentenced.' Rebecca Owens Vaul, Albert Owens' daughter, agreed: 'We are the ones that have been waiting 24 years for justice to be served. I find it beyond bad taste that the man that killed my father has been nominated for not one, but two Nobel Peace Prizes. I would like to be able to see my father's grave and tell him that the man that took him away from us has finally been brought to justice.'

Although Stanley and his supporters had maintained his innocence throughout—that he was railroaded and framed—every appeals court refused to buy it in the face of the evidence the prosecution presented. Even the Nobel Prize nominations didn't cut it. Critics argued that any college professor can nominate someone for the Nobel Peace Prize. Adolf Hitler, Josef Stalin and Benito Mussolini were all once nominees.

Nor did any arguments sway California's *Governator* Arnold Schwarznegger. In fact no California Governor has granted clemency to any Death Row inmate since Ronald Reagan in 1967. On 8 December 2005 Schwarznegger held a clemency hearing, which in the end turned out to be totally pointless. The only grounds on which a governor would grant clemency is innocence, yet although Stanley always claimed such innocence, critics maintain that he never renounced gang membership, nor did he ever provide contrary testimony on who actually did the killings, if in fact, it wasn't him.

In the face of all the controversy, Linda Owens, Albert Owens' widow made this statement:

> 'I, Linda Owens want to build upon Mr Williams' peace initiative. I invite Mr. Williams to join me in sending a message to all communities that we should all unite in peace. This position of peace would honour my husband's memory and Mr Williams' work.'

On 13 December, Governor Schwarznegger denied clemency for Stanley. He cited many reasons, among them that the alleged irregularities in his trial had been thoroughly examined but:

> 'Cumulatively, the evidence demonstrating Williams is guilty of these murders is strong and compelling. Furthermore: Is Williams' redemption complete and sincere, or is it just a hollow promise? Stanley Williams insists he is innocent, and that he will not and should not apologise or otherwise atone for the murders of the four victims in this case. Without an apology and atonement for these senseless and brutal killings there can be no redemption. In this case, the one thing that would be the clearest indication of complete remorse and full redemption is the one thing Williams will not do.'

It seems odd to ask Stanley to atone for crimes he maintains he did not commit, yet apparently, that's the only thing that could have saved him.

On 13 December 2005, Stanley Williams died by lethal injection at San Quentin State Prison in Marin County. He had had no last meal. He was declared dead at 12:35 am—the first Californian street gang member to be executed. Reports say that it took operators about 20 minutes to insert the needles.

His last words were recorded and later played at his funeral:

> 'The war within me is over. I battled my demons and I was triumphant. Teach them how to avoid our destructive footsteps. Teach them to strive for higher education. Teach them to promote peace and teach them to focus on rebuilding the neighbourhoods that you, others and I helped to destroy.'

He had two sons by his ex-wife Bonnie Williams Taylor. Travon Williams is a married father and homeowner who works for social services in Los Angeles. The younger son, Stanley 'Little Tookie' Williams IV, a Neighbourhood Crip, is serving 16 years in jail for the second-degree gang retaliation murder of a twenty-year-old woman in an alley off Sunset Boulevard.

Raymond Washington, founder of the East Side Crips, was shot to death in August 1979. No-one was ever arrested for his murder.

***

On 13 January, 2006 Carla Andrews, a long-time friend of Stanley wrote:

> 'Although he was known by everyone as Tookie, I honour his request to use his Christian name, Stanley Williams. As Mr. Williams once stated, "Tookie died a long time ago."
>
> I am writing this exactly one month from the date Stanley Williams was killed by the State of California. When I first founded Battle Cry Of Innocence I made the decision not to work with Death Row prisoners. Why? Because I knew it was inevitable that someone I worked with would be executed. But my desire to protect myself was quickly overridden by the Death Row cases of injustice I encountered, one of the first being Stanley Williams. Then on 13 December 2005, my worst fear became a reality.
>
> I consider Stanley Williams to be the "poster child" of why the Death Penalty does not work. Was he proven guilty beyond

> a reasonable doubt? I believe he was convicted because of his notoriety, not hard evidence of guilt. A trial riddled with inconsistencies, contradictions, lack of physical evidence, a racist prosecutor and wild stories from snitches and co-defendants trying to save their own necks, point to the possibility that Mr Williams may have been railroaded by a system hell-bent on keeping the Crips gang's founder off the streets. Stanley Williams steadfastly maintained his innocence from day one, even knowing that by doing so he was greatly minimising his chance of being granted clemency. But regardless of guilt or innocence, Mr Williams is the epitome of what the system claims to be striving for … REHABILITATION!

In reality, prisons have become big business and are being misused as a Band-Aid "solution" to social, political and economic problems. The system is set up to maintain the status quo of prisons, punishment, inhumanity and revenge upon the backs of those it fails the most. Stanley Williams never claimed to be a saint, but he undeniably proved that people can change. If the State of California had commuted Williams' sentence to life in prison he could have continued to use his influence to deter gang violence, thereby saving countless lives. His death didn't save any lives. It was about revenge, plain and simple.

The Death Penalty simply creates more victims and perpetrates the cycle of violence. I believe that there are two types of people who support the Death Penalty:

1. those who don't understand its inequities and
2. those who believe that revenge murder is acceptable. I, for one, will not rest until all people are educated about the racist, class-oriented and arbitrary Death Penalty and it is abolished across the nation. As Samuel Adams so eloquently stated, "It does not require a majority to prevail, but rather an irate tireless minority keen to set brush fires in people's mind."

Stanley Williams' legacy will not die with him. Rest in peace my friend.'

Coda: The Voices of Death Row

So what's Death Row really like? What does it mean to become someone who ends up there and, once there, what does it mean to be there, day after day, month after month, year after year?

During the writing of this book I made contact with several prisoners on Death Row.

I've made only very minimal changes to the letters they sent me.

Here they are.

William van Poyck

Bill has the rather dubious distinction of being, possibly, the only person on Death Row in America who, though admittedly guilty of the crime that he committed, didn't actually kill anyone. The story of his crimes, if not his whole life, is a testament to the often bizarre, inconsistent, arbitrary and arguably dysfunctional nature of not only America's legal system but also that of any legal system.

I was born in Miami, Florida on 18 September 1954, the third child of Walter Stuart van Poyck and Phyllis Herland van Poyck. My father was an executive with Eastern Airlines and my mother was a registered nurse. My father joined the US Army in September 1941 and was commissioned as a second lieutenant in the then new 82nd airborne. When America entered World War II, he participated in the invasions of North Africa, Sicily, Italy and France. In September 1944 after parachuting into Holland, Dad's leg was blown off by a German mortar. Dad was a captain at the time, a highly decorated company commander.

He spent the next two years at Walter Reed Memorial Hospital, in Washington D C, where he first met my mother. Phyllis, as a nurse, was taking care of my dad. After they married they moved to Miami, Florida. My older brother, Jeffrey, born on 18 June 1948, was my parents' first child. Next was my sister, Lisa, born on 15 July 1955. I was the last child born.

In January 1956, my mother went to our next-door neighbour's house to look after them, as the entire family was ill with what a doctor had told them with the flu. Unknown to the family they were actually suffering from carbon monoxide poisoning. Their father had stuffed up their gas heaters flue, to keep out the cold air. My mother decided to sleep overnight with the family because they were not recovering. On 16 January 1956, my father went next door to get my mom when she failed to show up for breakfast. My dad found the entire family dead, including my mom, from carbon monoxide poisoning. I was 16 months' old at this time.

My mother's death had a profound effect upon my brother, Jeff, who was seven years old. He became angry at life, very rebellious and perpetually acting out. For the next five years, we three children were taken care of by a series of housekeepers, each one successively worse. Each housekeeper was either a drunk or emotionally unstable or physically abusive or all of the above. Jeffrey reacted by staying away from the house as much as possible, roaming the neighbourhood, shoplifting candy from stores, living an unsupervised life. Lisa and I, being smaller, were stuck at home while dad worked all day and much of the night. We were often beaten and abused especially by our last housekeeper, Mrs Dano, who beat us almost every day and often locked us in the dark closet all day long.

In late 1960, my father married Lee Hightower and suddenly we three kids had a new stepmother, and a stepsister, Toni, who was Lee's daughter. This did not go well and was probably the most influential event in my life and not for a good reason. Lee was very strict, a severe disciplinarian, which clashed with my own stubborn and headstrong personality. Jeff hated Lee, and he recruited Lisa and I to hate her also, a task made easier by Lee's penchant to whip us with a belt and to punish us almost daily.

All three of us kids became increasingly rebellious, and Jeff became more criminal minded. Jeff began breaking into houses, late at night (he was 15, 16, 17, at this time), and when I was around nine or 10 and Jeff began taking me along with him on these burglaries, teaching me how to break into houses. Eventually, Jeff was caught and sent to Youth Hall, which began his 45-year history of incarcerations.

In 1966, when I was 11 and Lisa was 12, I began breaking into homes myself and I took Lisa along with me. We broke into many, many homes during the summer of 1966, until we were finally caught and sent to Youth Hall. From there we were sent to Kendall Children's Home, where we spent about a year locked up. When I got out, I stayed out of trouble for a while, but eventually I began breaking into houses again. I was eventually caught and sent to Okeehobee Boys School, where I spent the next several years. I kept escaping from Okeehobee, which is why I spent so much time there. From age 11 to 17, I spent over four years locked up.

In October 1971, I robbed a cashier in a restaurant, at gunpoint. I was eventually arrested for this and was convicted at a jury trial in January 1972. I was immediately sentenced to life imprisonment. I was 17 years old. I spent the next 15 years in prison, mostly in maximum-security prisons (seven years at Florida State Prison "FSP", the main maximum security prison in the state of Florida). I stayed in trouble in prison and I escaped numerous times.

The prisons I was in were very violent, lots of stabbings and murders. There was a lot of racially motivated violence and I endured several serious race riots. I had to become tough and brutal to survive. At the same time, I got my high school diploma, took many college courses, became a certified legal aid (paralegal) and became one of the best in-jailhouse lawyers in the Florida prison system. After 15 years, I was finally paroled, at age 32, in October 1986.

Some nine months later, on 24 June 1987, I, along with my friend Frank Valdes, attempted to free my best friend, James O'Brien, from a prison transport van in downtown West Palm Beach, Florida. During this incident Frank shot and killed one of the two prison guards (which was not part of the plan). After a high-speed car chase, during which I shot up four police cars, and after Frank crashed us into a tree, we were arrested. Eventually, we were both convicted and both sentenced to death. We spent the next 10 years on Death Row at Florida State Prison.

During my first three years I was kept in a super isolated maximum security cell, often in the dark, with no ventilation, no out-of-cell recreation, the solid door shut and sealed up, and no visits. I finally won a lawsuit and was placed on a regular Death Row wing.

On 17 July 1999, a gang of eight Florida State Prison Guards attacked Frank Valdes in his cell and stomped and beat him to death. Eventually eight guards were arrested and charged with second-degree murder. The state was never really serious about convicting these guards. Four guards were tried first (with a guard testifying against the other guards) but they were acquitted. An ex-prison guard (a Lieutenant) sat on the jury. After the acquittal the state had dropped the charges against the other four guards. So nobody ever went to jail over Frank's murder.

As a result of Frank's murder and because of the public uproar, Governor Bush ordered me transferred to Virginia, ostensibly for my own protection from renegade guards who wanted to murder me too. I was transferred here to Virginia's Death Row in October 1999, almost six years ago, where I've remained ever since. I have now been on Death Row for about 17 years. My case will be in front of the United States Supreme Court soon and this will probably be my final appeal. The main issue in my case is the propriety of sentencing someone to death who did not kill anyone and did not intend for anyone to be killed.

As to how I spend my time, I'm always busy doing something. My days are always full. I work out (exercise), read, write and do a lot of legal work. I'm always doing something so my mind is active and engaged. I have written three books (two novels and an autobiography), two of which have been published. I've also had quite a few of my short stories published in various literary journals. I am an optimist by nature and I focus on positive things, on trying to better myself and evolve as a human being. I have an insatiable intellectual curiosity and consequently I read just about everything I can get a hold of. I subscribe to about 30 different magazines (from current events, to history, to archaeology, to boating, to aviation, to architecture) and I read dozens of books a year, from the metaphysical to history to fiction. I watch some TV (mostly news, current events or nature shows) and I love music. I don't dwell on my future (whether I'll be executed or not) but instead focus on the here and now, on maturing, growing and evolving spiritually, mentally and emotionally. I have a website and I maintain a blog, which keeps me occupied and active.

I'm 51. Frank Valdes was 35 or 36 when he was murdered. I've been in institutions since age 11, more than 35 years, so to some degree I probably have become institutionalised. But I have no problem stepping out on the streets and fitting in. That's because while my body is inside, my mind is outside. I spend all of my time keeping my mind occupied on alert, I'm always writing, reading, studying, working out, doing legal work—things that keep my mind active. I don't dwell on prison, prison life or things going on inside these walls (though sometimes that can't be avoided).

Mike Ryan had nothing to do with anger. It was a simple plan to free my best friend. Obviously, it was poor judgment, to say the least that at the time I believed I could get away with it and I felt that I owed it to my friend. The only thing that stopped me from going straight was my lack of patience, combined with a lack of imagination. I went straight for three or four months, but I could only get minimum wage jobs doing physical labour (due to being an ex-convict) and I got tired of being perpetually broke. After just serving 15 years and enduring all that deprivation, I felt that I should have been doing better, once free, than living constantly on the edge of poverty.

My father died (heart attack) in December 1972, right after I went to prison at age 17, with a life sentence for robbery. My stepmother died a couple of years ago. Toni died about eight years ago. Lisa lives in Las Vegas, where she is an accountant. My brother Jeffrey is in federal prison for bank robbery.

I love my father and I don't have any hard feelings about him marrying Lee (my stepmom). Dad did the best that he could, the best that he knew how to do. Dad felt like Lee would bring some stability into our chaotic situation. And we three kids bear some responsibility. We were headstrong and rebellious, a real handful.

After living in/within the American criminal justice system for more than 35 years I know it to be very corrupt, very violent and very, very counterproductive. There is no attempted rehabilitation or education. This system seems deliberately designed to guarantee the released inmates will return to prison. This system breeds and engenders hatred and violence. Corrections is very big business in America and a large segment of corrections officials do not want to see it change. They want prisons to remain large, numerous and full, in order to guarantee lots of jobs. A lot of politicians feel the same way. Building and staffing prisons brings a lot of stable jobs to the communities and those workers vote for those politicians.

I was in the most violent prisons in Florida for many years. I had to carry a knife at all times, for many years. I had to fight a lot and I had to be mentally and physically prepared to kill at a moment's notice. I lived in a heightened state like that for years, witnessing many brutal murders and other violence. It was a constant struggle to maintain my humanity and sense of compassion. I was always fighting against the urge or tendency to devolve into a brute, to become the animal that society had consigned me to being. I learned to understand how and why some guys leave prisons like these and become mass murderers. That is their way to exact revenge on a faceless society which buried them in such violent, hopeless prisons without regard to the outcome. You reap what you sow and, when that happens, society is reaping what it sowed. I could easily become one of those people and it was only through a conscious act of will power that I did not do so.

Your friend,
Bill
13 July 2005—Wednesday evening and 15 October 2005—Saturday evening.

Milo Rose

Milo's story is one of chaos. Piecing together his story is like trying to put together a puzzle where the pieces seem to come from different pictures. Here are extracts from various statements and letters. Although the facts of the case are important, what's more important is that the writings below give you a very real sense of the emotional reality in which he lives. His words reveal a stark honesty about how he sees his predicament and provide us with the rare privilege of looking into the heart of someone in extraordinary circumstances.

Siyu, which is the Cherokee salutation for 'Hello'.

My name is Milo Andrew Rose, but I prefer to be called by my Native American name: One Eagle.

Since my arrest in October of 1982 I have given the legal system every opportunity to correct itself. Since it has repeatedly failed, it cannot be counted on to correct itself. I now welcome the opportunity to present the facts, which the legal system—thus far—has been successful in suppressing. When I stood midway through the farce and mockery called my trial and shouted to the jury that I was being railroaded, it was an act of pure desperation. I knew at this point, beyond any reasonable doubt, the court was not interested in the truth; that I had already been found guilty, with the twelve-member jury of my peers unwittingly playing the role of dupes.

***

Imagine being put on trial for the murder of your friend and the truth is suppressed so it appears you are overwhelmingly guilty. You are unable to put on a defence because you are not being told or given the truth and facts. So a jury of your peers looks at you in shock and amazement when you jump up mid-way through the trial and shout to them that you are being railroaded. But it is to no avail. The odds have been stacked against you. The jury only hears one side and that is the side told by your oppressors, who demonstrate no respect for the facts and truth, leaving the jury no choice but to convict and sentence you to death ...

This type of scenario is not supposed to happen in America. In this country a person is innocent until proven guilty. Yet in my case, as you will read, kangaroo courts and railroad jobs are not a thing of the past.

What is more shocking is that in this country's zeal to declare "War on Crime", it has shown total disregard for individual constitutional rights. Like some Death Row advocates have declared: it is totally acceptable to kill an innocent person as long as no guilty person escapes.

Now imagine yourself to be that innocent person. Is it acceptable with you to be that innocent casualty of the War on Crime? I never volunteered for the role of dupe in sacrificing myself and cannot imagine anyone else doing it either. So it should shock your moral conscience as to how few people care that the core of this country's moral fibre is corrupted to the extent that it does knowingly execute innocent people in the name of God and country.

★★★

I was kept in an isolation cell with the lights on 24 hours a day. To add to the sleep deprivation, the cell was kept cold until I went to sleep. Then it seems the vent above my bunk would blow out hot air and I'd wake up sweating and I'd be soaking wet or they would come find a reason to wake me up so I didn't get as much sleep as usual. Then I'd be shackled with leg irons and handcuffed whenever they took me out of the cell. I was forced to walk the distance of at least a half mile (800m)—I'm serious about the distance—with the heavy leg irons digging into my ankles. I done that four times, going and coming from the Court building. Every day I went through a similar routine but not as far, far enough I'd be in pain though. To use the telephone I'd have to walk about a block like that and then be locked in a small room that was like being in an icebox. If I was able to get someone on the phone my time would get cut short and if I wasn't able to get anyone I'd have to sit there and wait for them to return me to my cell. I didn't have a regular bowel movement all the time I was there too. Oh, I did get to read about 10 books though, thanks to one of the runners (Trustees) and one of the books I read was Steppenwolf by Hesse and I enjoyed it as I took it as a good sign. I'm still looking forward to reading Siddhartha, hint, hint.

***

My state appointed attorney's tactic of pleading an intoxication defence (without my knowledge or approval, see below) has backfired. I have been denied a new hearing and I feel that my claim of innocence, maintained for 18 years, has been recklessly compromised by their actions.

***

June 10th 2005
The Honourable Jeb Bush
Governor of Florida
The Capital
Tallahassee, Florida 32399

Dear Governor Bush,
Once more I find myself appealing for your compassion as the executive legal administer for the State of Florida, to preserve and protect the integrity of the law, through the signing of my second death warrant.

You have the power to help me expeditiously correct the grave miscarriage of justice I have suffered for nearly 23 years as an innocent man, wrongly convicted and sentenced to death.

The record of my case clearly reflects that I was rendered with ineffective assistance of counsel before and at trial, due to the prosecutorial misconduct of withheld exculpatory evidence in each aspect of the case presented against me. The record also clearly reflects the State of Florida is guilty of rendering me with self-proclaimed ineffective assistance of counsel thereafter, which the record will also clearly reflect, prevented me from fully developing the initial prosecutorial misconduct that would, and will demand my conviction and sentence be overturned. If I were not certain of these facts, I would not be making my third formal request to have my death warrant signed.

I do know from experience that the legal system is not designed to correct itself. I also know from experience that it won't, until it is placed under scrutiny. You signing my death warrant will assure the desired scrutiny takes place.

I pray you will honour my request!

***

I am an indigent Death Row inmate who happens to be innocent. I have been on Death Row since July 1983 and am just now coming to terms with my anger—an anger I allowed to consume me and become blind, as I transferred onto just about everyone. I suppose the profundity of growing out of control can be contributed to the fact of the nightmarish torture that began upon my arrest in October 1982. Continuing now for over 23 years with the knowledge that, if I am unable to gain the needed support to end this nightmare, it will continue for many more years.

Milo Rose, Sunday 13 November 2005.

As indeed it will for thousands of other cases. Meanwhile men and women continue to live, and die, on Death Row.

Selected Bibliography

The following sources are highly recommended:

AUSTRALIAN CASES

Kidd,Paul B, *Australia's Serial Killers: The Definitive History of Serial Multicide in Australia*, Pan Macmillan, Sydney, 2000.

Kidd,Paul B, *The Australian Crime File*, Five Mile Press, Sydney, 2005.

EDGAR ERIC COOKE

Blackburn, E, *Broken Lives*, Tower Books, 1998.

JEAN LEE

Wilson P, Treble D and Lincoln R, Jean Lee: The Last Woman Hanged in Australia, Random House, 1997.

This is the definitive account of the case. The authors argue that Lee's case is one that demonstrates how far women can be exploited in a system dominated by men.

Albiston J, *The Hanging of Jean Lee*, Poem, Black Pepper, 1998.

VAN TUONG NGUYEN

The full transcript of the case (from which I have quoted extensively) can be found at:

http://www.geocities.com/law4u2003/nguyentuongyan.htm

BRITISH CASES

Eddleston J J, *The Encyclopaedia of Executions*, John Blake, London, 2004.

Engel H, *Crimes of Passion*, Robson Books, London, 2004.

JOHN CHRISTIE

The 'definitive' works on the Christie/Evans case are:

Kennedy, L, *10 Rillington Place*, Panther Books, 1971.

Eddowes, J, *The Two Killers of Rillington Place*, Little, Brown, New York, 1994.

Ruth Ellis

Ellis, G, *Ruth Ellis: My Mother*, Smith Gryphon, 1996.
Jakubait, M, *Ruth Ellis: My Sister's Secret Life,* Robinson.

American Cases

Ted Bundy

Kendall, L, *The Phantom Prince, My Life with Ted Bundy*, Madrona, 1981.
Rule, A, *The Stranger Beside Me*, Signet, New York, 1980.

HH Holmes

Detective Frank P Geyer's book is available on CD-ROM from Waterfront Productions.
Erik Larson, E, *The Devil in the White City,* Vintage/Random House, 2004. Taylor, T, *Haunted Chicago—http://www.prairieghosts.com/chicago.html*

Albert Fish

Schechter, H, *The Shocking True Story of America's Most Fiendish Killer!*, Warner Books, London, 1992.
Film, *Wisteria,* scheduled for release in 2006.

John Wayne Gacy

Gacy, JW, *They Call Him Mr Gacy: Selected Correspondence of John Wayne Gacy,* Grindhouse Graphics, 1989.
Gacy, JW, *A Question of Doubt,* Craig Bowley Consultants, 1995.

Milo Rose

Read more of Milo's story, in his own words at:
http://zafu.demon.co.uk/milorose/milorose.htm

Ronald Joseph Ryan

Richards, M, *The Hanged Man: The Life and Death of Ronald Ryan*, Scribe Publishing, 2003.

William van Poyck

van Poyck, W, *A Checkered Past,* Author House, 2003.
van Poyck, W, *Quietus,* Author House, 2004.
Read more about Bill at his websites and blogs:
www.deathrowwriter.com

www.deathrowdiary.blogspot.com
www.deathrowspeaks.info

WASHINGTON SNIPERS

The Washington Post has an extensive and detailed website on the continuing story of the Washington Snipers.
Visit: *http://www.washingtonpost.com/wp-dyn/metro/specials/shootings/2002*

TOOKIE WILLIAMS

For a detailed history of Tookie Williams and the LA Crips, visit:
http://www.streetgangs.com/magazine/102605tookie.php
Information for all his books can be found at:
http://www.tookie.com/
You can access the complete *Los Angeles County District Attorney's Response to Stanley William's Petition for Executive Clemency* at:
http://www.lacountyda.org/pdf/swilliams.pdf

GENERAL REFERNCE

Abbott, G, *Execution: A Guide to the Ultimate Penalty*, Summersdale Publishers, 2005.
Death Row Volumes 1–9, a collection of magazine-style books published Glen Hare Publications and later by Bobit Publishing in California between 1991 and 1999. They are now out of print but you can still get back copies through the *Police Magazine* website:
http://www.policemag.com/mstore/
Macinnis, P, *The Killer Bean of Calabar and Other Stories*, Allen and Unwin, Crows Nest, 2004.
Vronsky, P, *Serial Killers*, Berkeley Books, New York, 2004.

DEATH ROW NOTES INTERNET SITES

The Internet provides a wealth of information from amateur and professional criminal historians.

As the first stop I would recommend:
http://www.clarkprosecutor.org/html/links/dplinks.htm

This site, set up by Clark County in Indiana, contains links to more than a thousand other death penalty related sites. Although parts of it have not been updated since September 2004, it's still a great place to start.
The Pro-Death Penalty Website: *http://www.prodeathpenalty.com/* is one of the few sites set up by those in favour of the death penalty and offers an important 'alternative' point of view.

The Death Penalty Information Centre Site:
http://www.deathpenaltyinfo.org/ is probably one of the best on the net and could easily provide you with days of reading.
Rob Gallagher's site, *Before the Needles*, is an extensive and almost exhaustive labour of love that gives accurate information for all executions in America prior to the introduction of lethal injection and the reintroduction of capital punishment in America in 1977:
http://users.bestweb.net/~rg/execution.htm

Capital Punishment UK:
http://www.richard.clark32.btinternet.co.uk/contents.html
and Capital Punishment USA: *http://www.geocities.com/trctl11/* provide interesting historical data too as does: *http://www.deathrow-usa.com/*.
Court TV's *The Crime Library* website is a wonderful source of case studies from professional crime writers, and is definitely worth a virtual trip or two: *http://www.crimelibrary.com/*

Another labour of love, or of passion, in the spirit of *Before The Needles* is: *http://people.smu.edu/rhalperi/* Rick Halperin's site gives you up-to-date information on past, current and pending executions.
Those interested in the legal issues of capital punishment can subscribe to *Capital Defence Weekly* at:
capital_defence_weekly-subscribe@yahoogroups.com or look up the archives at: *http://capitaldefenceweekly.com/index.html*

The Canadian Coalition Against the Death Penalty: *http://www.ccadp.org/* offers condemned prisoners the opportunity to set up their own web sites and is a nice place to start if you want to write to people on Death Row.

If you want to know about the woman who inspired the film *Dead Man Walking* then visit Helen Prejean's site: *http://www.prejean.org/*.

On the lighter side, consider the award-winning site *Dead Man Eating* for the latest on last meals: *http://www.deadmaneating.com/*.

For the official point of view from the top three executing states in America start with Texas: *http://www.tdcj.state.tx.us/stat/deathrow.htm*. Virginia: *http://www.vadoc.state.va.us/default.htm* has a rather stark virtual tour of a maximum-security prison cell and prison. Virginians though, seem remarkably coy about their executions and you won't find any mention on their official site. For that, you'll need to visit the very unofficial: *http://www.vadp.org/info.htm*.

The prize for official state sites must go to Florida: *http://www.dc.state.fl.us/oth/deathrow/index.html*. Its site is extensive, comprehensive and detailed, although California is a close runner-up and reveals quite a lot about procedures of execution in its site: *http://www.corr.ca.gov/CommunicationsOffice/CapitalPunishment/lethal_injection.asp*

If you want to listen to something truly extraordinary, visit: *http://www.soundportraits.org/on-air/execution_tapes/* The state of Georgia for many years actually recorded some of their executions as well as the last words of condemned criminals. It makes for fascinating listening. (You'll need to have RealPlayer™ installed on your computer.)

Some remarkable sites created by people supporting prisoners on Death Row:
Death Row Speaks—http://www.deathrowspeaks.info/ and
Battlecry of Innocence—http://www.battlecryofinnocence.com/
Both sites are run entirely by dedicated volunteers and are recommended if you want to make contact with prisoners living on Death Row.

Xavier Waterkeyn, February 2006.